New
Daylight

Edited by Naomi Starkey   May–August 2013

7   The Benedictus (Luke 1:67–79)
      Margaret Silf   1–7 May

15   Making disciples of all nations
      Stephen Rand   8–23 May

32   Bible stories rediscovered: Samson
      Rosie Ward   24 May–3 June

44   'I call you friends'
      Helen Julian CSF   4–17 June

59   2 Kings 9—12
      David Winter   18–29 June

72   1 and 2 Timothy
      Andrew John   30 June–20 July

94   Jesus' wisdom in Luke 13—16
      Liz Hoare   21 July–3 August

109   Stephen's speech (Acts 7:2–53)
      Naomi Starkey   4–17 August

124   Aidan, Cuthbert and Lindisfarne
      Barbara Mosse   18–31 August

139   The BRF Magazine

New Daylight © BRF 2013

The Bible Reading Fellowship
15 The Chambers, Vineyard, Abingdon OX14 3FE
Tel: 01865 319700; Fax: 01865 319701
E-mail: enquiries@brf.org.uk; Website: www.brf.org.uk

ISBN 978 1 84101 762 4

Distributed in Australia by Mediacom Education Inc., PO Box 610, Unley, SA 5061.
Tel: 1800 811 311; Fax: 08 8297 8719;
E-mail: admin@mediacom.org.au
Available also from all good Christian bookshops in Australia.
For individual and group subscriptions in Australia:
Mrs Rosemary Morrall, PO Box W35, Wanniassa, ACT 2903.

Distributed in New Zealand by Scripture Union Wholesale, PO Box 760, Wellington
Tel: 04 385 0421; Fax: 04 384 3990; E-mail: suwholesale@clear.net.nz

Publications distributed to more than 60 countries

Acknowledgments

Printed in Singapore by Craft Print International Ltd

Suggestions for using *New Daylight*

Find a regular time and place, if possible, where you can read and pray undisturbed. Before you begin, take time to be still and perhaps use the BRF prayer. Then read the Bible passage slowly (try reading it aloud if you find it over-familiar), followed by the comment. You can also use *New Daylight* for group study and discussion, if you prefer.

The prayer or point for reflection can be a starting point for your own meditation and prayer. Many people like to keep a journal to record their thoughts about a Bible passage and items for prayer. In *New Daylight* we also note the Sundays and some special festivals from the Church calendar, to keep in step with the Christian year.

New Daylight and the Bible

New Daylight contributors use a range of Bible versions, and you will find a list of the versions used opposite, on page 2. You are welcome to use your own preferred version alongside the passage printed in the notes, and this can be particularly helpful if the Bible text has been abridged.

New Daylight affirms that the whole of the Bible is God's revelation to us, and we should read, reflect on and learn from every part of both Old and New Testaments. Usually the printed comment presents a straight-forward 'thought for the day', but sometimes it may also raise questions rather than simply providing answers, as we wrestle with some of the more difficult passages of Scripture.

New Daylight *is also available in a deluxe edition (larger format). Check out your local Christian bookshop or contact the BRF office, who can also give more details about a cassette version for the visually impaired. For a Braille edition, contact St John's Guild, 8 St Raphael's Court, Avenue Road, St Albans, AL1 3EH.*

3

Writers in this issue

Margaret Silf is an ecumenical Christian, committed to working across and beyond the denominational divides. She devotes herself to writing and accompanying others on their spiritual journey.

Stephen Rand is a writer and speaker who travelled widely with Tearfund for many years, and now shares his time between persecuted church charity Open Doors and Fresh Streams—a largely Baptist church leaders network. He and his wife Susan live in Oxfordshire.

Rosie Ward was ordained in 1994, has served in three varied parishes and worked as a Leadership Development Adviser at CPAS. She has written several booklets and books, including *Growing Women Leaders* (BRF/CPAS, 2008).

Helen Julian CSF has been a member of the Community of St Francis, an Anglican Franciscan community of women, since 1985, and is presently serving as Minister General. She has written several books for BRF, including *The Road to Emmaus*.

David Winter is retired from parish ministry. An honorary Canon of Christ Church, Oxford, he is well known as a writer and broadcaster. His most recent book for BRF is *Facing the Darkness and Finding the Light*.

Andrew John has been the Bishop of Bangor since 2008, having previously served all his ministry in the Diocese of St Davids. He is married to Caroline, who is also a deacon in the Church in Wales, and they have four children.

Liz Hoare is tutor in prayer and pastoral studies at Wycliffe Hall, Oxford. She has a special interest in Celtic and desert spiritualities and a deep commitment to accompanying people in prayer. She is married to Toddy, an ordained Anglican priest and sculptor, and they have one son.

Naomi Starkey is a Commissioning Editor for BRF and edits and writes for *New Daylight* Bible reading notes. She has also written *The Recovery of Love* (BRF, 2012).

Barbara Mosse is an Anglican priest with experience in prison, university, community mental health and hospital chaplaincies. She has lectured on the MA in Christian Spirituality at Sarum College, Salisbury. She is the author of *Encircling the Christian Year* (BRF, 2012).

Naomi Starkey writes...

As Messy Church continues to flourish around the world, I have sometimes wondered whether the whole 'messy' concept could be usefully extended to other areas of BRF's ministry! This fantastic mission initiative gathers people for worship who might not normally consider going near a regular Sunday service. It broadcasts the fact that church should not be a club for the tidy, the sorted-out, the élite, but for ordinary families who are, quite often, messy in all kinds of ways. From time to time, though, isolated voices disagree with the name 'Messy Church'. For them, church should equate not with mess but only with order, harmony, beauty and quiet...

While I doubt that we will end up as the Messy Bible Reading Fellowship, it is occasionally worth challenging our preconceptions about the 'tidiness' of the Bible. We can be so familiar with the beautifully bound book, perhaps in an edition customised to our interests, gender or age, that we forget the long history of its development, the remoteness of so many of its settings, even the fact that it was not originally written in English (and some Old Testament vocabulary is particularly obscure in meaning). Even so, under the guidance of God's Spirit, the scriptures came together in their present form, while different parts of the church still disagree about the inclusion of certain books.

Messy Bible? Yes, in a way. Think of 2 Kings, which David Winter covers for us in this issue. As he points out, modern sensibilities can be severely tested by its bloodthirsty events. Then there is the story of Samson, anti-hero leader in ancient Israel, which Rosie Ward discusses. We should be wary of glossing over awkward bits (God apparently condoning violence) or failing to question long-standing interpretations (Delilah as evil seductress—or pawn in men's power games?).

Messy Bible? Yes, but then life is messy. The turbulent and unsettled times of Aidan of Lindisfarne, which Barbara Mosse invites us to explore, bear similarities to our own times. And the word of God that spoke so powerfully and transformatively then can still speak with power and transform us today. We just need to read it—and also be ready to listen to what God may be saying to us through it.

The BRF Prayer

Almighty God,
you have taught us that your word is a lamp for our feet
and a light for our path. Help us, and all who prayerfully
read your word, to deepen our fellowship with you
and with each other through your love.
And in so doing may we come to know you more fully,
love you more truly, and follow more faithfully
in the steps of your son Jesus Christ, who lives and reigns
with you and the Holy Spirit, one God for evermore.
Amen

The Benedictus (Luke 1:67–79)

We use blessings all the time. Someone sneezes and we say, 'Bless you', implicitly wishing them better health. We tuck a child up in bed or take leave of a friend with the words 'God bless!' We end a letter or e-mail with the simple wish 'Blessings!' We may express such blessings so automatically we barely think about them, but the blessing that accompanies us through this week is one which comes very much from the heart.

It is, first and foremost, one of the formal, ritualised Jewish benedictions (*berachot*) expressing thanksgiving that a divine commandment has been fulfilled. For Zechariah, the blessing is also a very personal one. God's promise has been fulfilled in his own life in a way that he initially dismissed as impossible. He and his wife, Elizabeth, childless and now beyond child-bearing age, have become the parents of John the Baptist. So dismissive was Zechariah of God's promise of this impending birth that God deprived him of his speech until such time as the promise would be fulfilled.

Now it has been fulfilled and lies in a cradle, the one who will become the herald of the coming Messiah. Zechariah's speech has been restored and we join him over the next seven days, sharing this ancient and beautiful prayer of thanksgiving—a prayer that can be heard daily in the office of Lauds or Morning Prayer.

It expresses gratitude and praise for the restoration of what has been lost, deliverance from what threatens us and the fulfilment of God's promise in our lives. It also calls us to become people who are blessed and pass on that blessing in service to God and others. It calls us forward to greet a new dawn, a new beginning.

We are all familiar with the story of Zechariah and Elizabeth and all that they want to bless God for, but what about ourselves? As we embark on our week with the Benedictus, let us pause to reflect on the question, 'In my life, God's promise is also being fulfilled in very specific ways. For what do I personally want to bless God?'

Margaret Silf

Beyond belief

Then his father Zechariah was filled with the Holy Spirit and spoke this prophecy: 'Blessed be the Lord God of Israel, for he has looked favourably on his people and redeemed them.'

Zechariah knew all the rules and doctrines of his faith. In fact, he could be described as an 'expert' about God and God's ways—a true believer. Both he and Elizabeth, his wife, were 'righteous before God, living blamelessly according to all the commandments and regulations of the Lord' (v. 6). God, though, took Zechariah by surprise with the astonishing news that his wife, in her old age, was to bear a son. God appeared to be holding out to him something that is humanly impossible. His response was a human one, full of doubts and questions (vv. 12–20).

The beliefs he held in his head were no help to him in this radically changed situation. God was calling him to do something beyond merely intellectual belief in the doctrines or even righteous living—that is, to trust in God's person. He was not yet ready to make 'the longest journey', that from his head to his heart. He was not yet able to step over the threshold that leads beyond belief to trust.

A story is told about a man who entertained the crowds by pushing a wheelbarrow across a high wire, over a deep abyss. He asked the crowds, 'Do you believe I can do this?' and they all shouted, 'Yes! We believe you can do this.' 'OK,' said the high wire walker, 'So who is going to get in the wheelbarrow?'

That is the difference between believing and trusting. Zechariah was initially unwilling to step into the wheelbarrow. Only when we trust will our heart become opened to God's power and God's new life. Only then will we be enabled to speak God's truth.

Today, as we begin our journey through the Benedictus, we encounter a new Zechariah. His heart has become open to God's promise, however startling and impossible that promise may seem, and his lips are ready, too, to express his response in this great hymn of praise.

Reflection

*May our hearts be open to God's 'impossibilities', so that we, too,
may sing God's blessing song.*

MARGARET SILF

A long continuum of love

'He has raised up a mighty saviour for us in the house of his servant David, as he spoke through the mouth of his holy prophets
from of old...'

The blessing that is celebrated in the Benedictus is one that emerges
from among us, from one like us. The fulfilment of God's promise happens here and now and in the place where we really are. For Zechariah
and his contemporaries, this means that the miracle reveals itself 'in the
house of David'. For us, this same miracle is inviting us to welcome its
power into our home, our place of work, our neighbourhood, our
generation.

'Incarnation' means exactly this: God with us where we really are,
not in some distant historical narrative but in the present moment, with
all its difficulties and dilemmas, tears and laughter. Nevertheless, God's
promise has its roots deep in the human story, way back in the very
beginnings of time. It is the ongoing story of the outpouring of God's
love all through the ages. This salvation story has been reiterated
through the prophetic voices and through lives that have revealed
glimpses of its power and its glory. The fulfilment of God's promise is
imminent and its herald has already been conceived in the womb of one
whose husband thought such an event to be beyond the bounds of
possibility.

Zechariah has come to understand that the one who reveals the glory
of God in human form is coming to birth in a person we can relate to in
our ordinary lives and his own son John is to play a crucial role in preparing the way that will open up, in the birth of Jesus, for all humankind.

It is one long continuum, from the first utterance of God's promise,
through the holy prophets who heard this utterance in their hearts and
proclaimed it to the world, right through to its coming to birth in our
own lives.

Reflection

*May the one who is proclaimed rise up among us not only in the events
of 2000 years ago but also in the situations and circumstances of our
own lives, here and now.*

MARGARET SILF

Save us from ourselves

'… that we would be saved from our enemies and from the hand of all who hate us.'

For as long as human conflict has blighted life on earth, combatants have prayed to be delivered from their enemies. Perhaps our most oft-repeated prayer is to be saved from whatever threatens us, and that is Zechariah's prayer today. From what exactly do we beg to be delivered? Where is the enemy and whose are the hands of those who hate us?

In her 2011 Christmas address, Queen Elizabeth II, reflecting on the birth of Jesus, suggested that frequently our need is to be saved from ourselves. Like many of us, she can look back over many decades of world history, including times of overwhelming darkness and deprivation as well as highlights of joy, and recognise, in hindsight, how global conflict often begins in the individual heart.

The Benedictus today reminds us of God's promise to deliver us from all that threatens us, but what if our greatest enemy lurks within our own hearts and the hand that does us the worst harm is our own? We may, for example, need to be saved from selfish attitudes that are alienating us from our friends and eroding our relationships. We may need to be saved from unnecessary fears that are making us intolerant of people whose ideas we do not understand or agree with. We may need to be saved from a short temper or from a long memory for past grievances.

Gerard Hughes—much-loved spiritual writer and activist for justice and peace—was once asked in an interview, 'If you could ask God to bring peace to any one conflict zone in the world today, which would it be?' He replied, without a moment's hesitation, 'My own heart.' The most intractable area of conflict is the human heart and no one is an exception to this truth. Very few of us have any real influence over international affairs. It is in our own hearts that God's promise can begin to be fulfilled, but only if we both desire it and permit it.

Reflection

Dare I ask God to save me from myself? What would such a prayer uncover in my own conflicted heart?

MARGARET SILF

The quality of mercy

'Thus he has shown the mercy promised to our ancestors, and has remembered his holy covenant, the oath that he swore to our ancestor Abraham...'

Yesterday, we were reminded that God's promise is to deliver us from what threatens us, especially when the greatest threat we face is the enemy within our own hearts. Today, a different, but related, promise is revealed—the promise of mercy. My first exposure to the work of William Shakespeare was the study of his play *The Merchant of Venice* when I started high school. Many of us will have learned the most famous quotation from this play: 'The quality of mercy is not strained. / It droppeth as the gentle rain from heaven / upon the place beneath: it is twice blest; / it blesseth him that gives and him that takes.'

Today, the Benedictus echoes this truth about the blessing: it works two ways. We are blessed by God's mercy and blessed again when we show to others the quality of mercy God bestows on us. To live true to God's promise in our own hearts—the promise that people of faith have trusted since the time of Abraham onwards—we are asked to be people of mercy, reflecting the merciful God in whose image we are created. Mercy is a foundational principle of God's reign; the kingdom is a kingdom of mercy. It was so from the very beginning, encoded into the holy covenant between God and God's people. What, though, does mercy mean in our own lives?

We show mercy when we hold back from making a sarcastic comment about someone who has just said or done something foolish. We show mercy when, instead of laughing at another person's mistake, we try to help them recover from it. Perhaps most difficult of all, we show mercy to ourselves when we stop driving ourselves to be perfect and allow ourselves, from time to time, to sit back, relax and enjoy a quiet hour with no pressure.

Reflection

May we learn to be people of mercy, passing on to others, including ourselves, the mercy that God has shown to us. In showing mercy, may we also know ourselves to be doubly blessed.

MARGARET SILF

Free to serve

'... to grant us that we, being rescued from the hands of our enemies, might serve him without fear, in holiness and righteousness before him all our days.'

Imagine a life without fear! Fear is love's great enemy. Fear of losing something we value—our possessions, our status, our position of power—can lead us to defend these things even to the point of attacking others or engaging in criminal activity. A fear of poverty or hunger can, understandably, make us defensive in other ways, perhaps by becoming greedy and hoarding more than we need or taking our own advantage at the expense of the common good. Fear of our neighbour can make us suspicious and distrustful, tending to assume the worst of our fellow human beings rather than envisioning the best that we can be. We can even project on to the people we live and work with the fears that are actually rooted in international events, so we begin to avoid normal human contact with some of those around us because they happen to come from a different culture or faith tradition than our own. This is not the voice of the gospel.

Imagine this scenario. Joanne has just moved into a new area where she is feeling very lost and timid among people of a different culture. Her fear shows in her eyes. As a result, others are a bit wary of her and nobody offers friendship. Soon, Joanne has convinced herself that the people in her new area are hostile. She remains aloof from her neighbours. Now suppose that Joanne could be freed from these fears. Perhaps someone breaks through with a kind or generous gesture. The barriers begin to fall. She starts to make friends. Soon she actually wants to give something to her new neighbourhood and begins to join in projects that will benefit those worse off than herself. She has been rescued from her fears and set free to serve God and her neighbours. Love has conquered fear.

Reflection

May we be set free from all our reasons to be fearful and liberated to love and serve God and each other, knowing that love shows itself in deeds of service, not just in words, however high-sounding they may be.

MARGARET SILF

Small is great

'And you, child, will be called the prophet of the Most High; for you will go before the Lord to prepare his ways, to give knowledge of salvation to his people by the forgiveness of their sins.'

I had an unexpected phone call the other day from an old friend. He was feeling a bit low and needed to talk. He was reflecting back over his life and feeling that he had not really achieved very much, in terms of making the world a better place. I reminded him that, as a publisher of books on Christian spirituality, he had actually changed lives without ever realising it. 'Yes, maybe,' he conceded, 'but in such small ways.'

'The gospel is all about "small ways",' I reminded him. Jesus speaks so much of small things, of seeds and grains of wheat, of a fragment of yeast, a single lost sheep from a large flock. It is we who expect grand and instant solutions, but God always seems to start small, with seeds tiny enough to plant in a single heart.

Zechariah echoes this thinking in today's passage, turning our normal expectations on their heads. A newborn child will become the one who will proclaim the coming of God, teaching his people about the One who is to come. Also, later, the one foretold at this point will call on all of us to become like little children and trust God to grow God's kingdom from these tiny seeds in our hearts.

My friend ended the conversation by telling me how he and his wife rejoice every time they hear Handel's *Messiah*. They recently adopted a little boy, whom they adore. When they hear the words 'Unto us a son is given', their hearts swell with love and soar in thanksgiving. Their son is called Gabriel—only a child, but still with the power to change their hearts and lives.

Reflection

The one who rests in God's blessing can see greatness in what appears to be very small. The one who brings God's blessing can see the possibilities that lie latent in you. We may not share such vision, due to our limited human understanding, but the Benedictus calls us to trust it.

MARGARET SILF

An everlasting dawn

'By the tender mercy of our God, the dawn from on high will break upon us, to give light to those who sit in darkness and in the shadow of death, to guide our feet into the way of peace.'

I will never forget the first time I flew into Africa. It was just after 5 a.m. Everything was pitch dark below us, but it was just possible to discern a faint ring of rose-gold light shaping itself around the curvature of the earth, like a ring of promise. Ever so gradually, the ring of light increased in intensity, as if urging the darkness to give birth to this new day. Just as the features of the earth below us began to take shape, the light of a new dawn roused all to life again.

When I read today's promise that 'the dawn from on high will break upon us', this experience leaps to mind. Just as the dawn from on high breaks over us every morning, revealing the details of our life on earth, so the spiritual light of God's love breaks into our hearts and minds, with the power to enlighten our choices and decisions and enliven all our relationships and actions.

Without the daybreak, the earth would remain in impenetrable darkness. Without the dawn of God's love into our lives, our hearts would remain unawakened and sterile. How does this happen in reality?

As we come to the end of our week with the Benedictus, we might pause to remember with gratitude the times when we personally know the touch of God's dawning light. Perhaps there have been other times when we were aware of God's guidance, accompanying us through a period of confusion and doubt. Perhaps an awareness of loving consolation broke through to us during an experience of loss or grief or else an invisible hand restrained us and led us beyond the conflicts in our lives into ways of peace. All of these were signs of the dawn from on high.

Reflection

Take a few moments to look back over your life. In what personal ways can you also sing that 'the dawn from on high' has broken in on your life?

MARGARET SILF

Making disciples of all nations

This topic is at the heart of what I have tried to live and teach over many years. Archbishop William Temple is reputed to have said that 'the church is the only society on earth that exists for the benefit of non-members'. Mission is the key task of the church as it fulfils the purposes of God.

Mission is not about getting converts, it is about *making disciples*. I'm passionately committed to evangelism, encouraging people to make a decision to follow Christ, but it has to be concerned with more than just that initial decision. It's vital to start the race... but equally vital to run it well and finish it. The task of mission is to build a community of disciples—people learning to live like Jesus as they follow him day by day.

Those disciples are to come *from all nations*. The Church is wonderfully, gloriously inclusive. No one is to be left out of the possibility of being part of this eternal worshipping community.

Our first passage reveals the Church gathered before the throne of God: 'from every nation, tribe, people and language' (Revelation 7:9). However you decide to divide up the human race, you will find that God has found a representative of every division and united them together in Christ. Whatever shape the piece of the jigsaw, it will be fitted into the whole to make the big picture.

'Nation' suggests the world of political division and diversity, but no border controls have been able to seal off a country from the good news of Jesus. 'Tribe' indicates ethnicity, but there is no place for racism here. 'People' hints at cultural identity, but the gospel is never defeated by culture, gloriously transforming it instead. 'Language'—all that amazing pioneering work done by translators, convinced that everyone has the right to read the word of God in their own language, has now been brought to fruition.

The passages that follow will take us through to Pentecost—the birthday of the Church—and beyond. If the mission to make disciples is the purpose of the Church, then the power, the energy, the dynamite for that mission comes from God's Spirit: 'you will receive power when the Holy Spirit comes on you; and you will be my witnesses in Jerusalem, and in all Judea and Samaria, and to the ends of the earth' (Acts 1:8).

Stephen Rand

Having the end in view

After this I looked, and there before me was a great multitude that no one could count, from every nation, tribe, people and language, standing before the throne and before the Lamb. They were wearing white robes and were holding palm branches in their hands. And they cried out in a loud voice: 'Salvation belongs to our God, who sits on the throne, and to the Lamb.'

I remember as a child going with my family to the Keswick Convention. I had grown up in a small, tightly knit church; now I was in a massive tent, witnessing a Communion service shared by thousands of people. It was, literally, a revelation—and, even if only slightly, it was a foretaste of heaven. An enormous crowd, from many different backgrounds and locations, worshipping together, united by their salvation that came through faith in the risen Christ who is also the sacrificial Lamb.

My father had attended the Keswick Convention as a young man with a friend who had sensed the call of God to become a missionary, to share the love of God with people who had never heard the name of Jesus. That friend was Geoffrey Bull and he arrived in Tibet just before it was engulfed by the Chinese Army. He was captured, imprisoned, tortured and, after three years, released. He visited our house when I was a young boy. He could not have looked less like a hero, but, in one sense, he was: he had risked his life because he thought people far away deserved the opportunity to come to faith and, one day, become part of the great celestial worship choir that John had seen in his vision 2000 years earlier.

Remember, we live in the heritage of equally heroic figures who risked all to travel to the inhospitable far reaches of the Roman Empire because they recognised that God could transform even the most barbaric tribes: 'not Angles, but angels', one of the first missionaries to Britain is reputed to have said.

Reflection

Whenever you feel isolated or lacking in faith, remember that, in Christ, you are part of a great company gathered throughout time and geography. Today, we have read the end of the book… and God wins.

STEPHEN RAND

Famous last words

Then they gathered round [Jesus] and asked him, 'Lord, are you at this time going to restore the kingdom to Israel?' He said to them: 'It is not for you to know the times or dates the Father has set by his own authority. But you will receive power when the Holy Spirit comes on you; and you will be my witnesses in Jerusalem, and in all Judea and Samaria, and to the ends of the earth.' After he said this, he was taken up before their very eyes, and a cloud hid him from their sight.

If you were making a final speech to the people you were closest to, you would probably say what you thought was the most important thing they should hear. The disciples were still focused on the political solution to Roman occupation, but, as Jesus prepared to leave them, his focus was on the task that God had set in motion by his birth, life, death and resurrection. It was the task that the disciples would be entrusted to complete, in the power of the Holy Spirit.

Jesus gives a clear pattern for mission. It begins at home (Jerusalem). It spreads to the places best known to us (Judea) and the ones we avoid because we distrust those who live there (Samaria). It goes far beyond our geographical and cultural comfort zones (the ends of the earth).

I have visited churches where the focus was entirely parochial; I have also visited one where there was great sadness that the Vietnamese refugees next door using the church kitchen had wrecked the annual missionary weekend! We need to be witnesses to those in our own community who are being overlooked, but also face the continuing challenge of the 'ends of the earth'. It is estimated that over 7000 people groups (40 per cent of the total) are 'unreached', with no Christian believers at all or too few to be able to share the gospel with their group without help from outside (www.joshuaproject.net).

Reflection

The Greek word translated 'witnesses' is the root word for 'martyr' in English. Many who heard these words of Jesus would become martyrs; some faithful witnesses here and now will share in that experience. Mission has its cost, but also its reward.

STEPHEN RAND

Pride leads to confusion

Now the whole world had one language and a common speech...
Then they said, 'Come, let us build ourselves a city, with a tower that
reaches to the heavens, so that we may make a name for ourselves;
otherwise we will be scattered over the face of the whole earth.'...
The Lord said, 'If as one people speaking the same language they
have begun to do this, then nothing they plan to do will be impossible
for them...' So the Lord scattered them from there over all the earth,
and they stopped building the city. That is why it was called Babel—
because there the Lord confused the language of the whole world.

I have travelled the world, but I am hopeless when it comes to languages. My French teacher told me my O level pass was a 'gross miscar-
riage of justice'. This Bible story gives me the excuse that I was fighting
against great odds! More importantly, it reinforces the biblical truth—
that human pride is met with God's judgment.

When The Shard, London's latest and tallest skyscraper was opened,
there was much comment about how the view of St Paul's Cathedral
had been overshadowed by a building symbolising wealth and power at
a time when both were all too readily identified with corruption and
pride. The human aspiration to 'make a name for ourselves' often leads
to exploitation and oppression.

Today's passage, then, is a difficult one. It seems to imply that God
was afraid of potential human achievement and stepped in to protect
himself. Perhaps, in fact, he was protecting humankind from the tyr-
anny of totalitarianism and enabling us to fulfil his intention for us to
fill the earth. The attempt to create unity by human endeavour without
reference to God resulted in disunity and confusion—babble. As we
shall see, however, God's mission to bring people back into fellowship
with him and one another will overcome the barrier of multiple languages by the power of his Spirit. The coming Day of Pentecost is a sign
that human pride will not, in the end, thwart God's purposes.

Prayer

Thank you for those who work to provide people with the Bible in their own
language. Grant fruit for their labours, we pray. Amen

STEPHEN RAND

The promise of blessing

The Lord had said to Abram, 'Go from your country, your people and your father's household to the land I will show you. I will make you into a great nation, and I will bless you; I will make your name great, and you will be a blessing. I will bless those who bless you, and whoever curses you I will curse; and all peoples on earth will be blessed through you.' So Abram went, as the Lord had told him.

It is one of life's great mysteries and also great joys that God *chooses* to use people to achieve his purposes. The one who made the universe by a simple word of command could actually manage without you and me, but such is his grace that he encourages and empowers us to work with him. The Christian can have no better reason for getting up in the morning.

This story, too, reveals a pattern for the way God works. It begins with a call from God—perhaps, more accurately, a command. The person responds positively, in terms of both obedience and faith. Abram is held up as just such an example of faith in the New Testament (Romans 4:13; Galatians 3:6–14; Hebrews 11:8).

Note that obedience to God produces blessing—for both the individual and, vitally, for others. Every blessing received is a blessing to be shared. In this case, you and I can benefit from Abram's obedience over 4000 years ago: 'everyone who has faith is a child of Abraham, [and] will share in the blessings that were given to Abraham because of his faith' (Galatians 3:7, 9, CEV).

If the Church is to be faithful to God's calling, it must share the blessings it has received with 'all peoples'. This has geographical implications—the Arctic Inuits and Auca Indians are 'sharers in the blessing' just as much as the British—and a sociological challenge—it applies to not just the financially and socially secure but also the single parents, those on benefits, the immigrants, everyone.

Prayer

We pray for all those who, like Abram, have been obedient to your call and left their country, homes and families to enable others to be blessed by the gospel of Jesus.

STEPHEN RAND

Global purpose, global praise

May God be gracious to us and bless us and make his face shine on us—so that your ways may be known on earth, your salvation among all nations. May the peoples praise you, God; may all the peoples praise you. May the nations be glad and sing for joy, for you rule the peoples with equity and guide the nations of the earth. May the peoples praise you, God; may all the peoples praise you. The land yields its harvest; God, our God, blesses us. May God bless us still, so that all the ends of the earth will fear him.

It is Sunday! When you woke up this morning there were those who had already gathered for worship, bringing their praise to God. It may have been in a vast church in America or a tiny shack in an Indian slum; it may have been in trembling and in secret in North Korea. When you go to bed, too, there will be people on the other side of the world about to sing for joy. As John Ellerton puts it in his hymn, 'The day thou gavest, Lord, is ended', 'And hour by hour fresh lips are making Thy wondrous doings heard on high.'

This is wonderful testimony to the work of God who prompted his disciples to go to the ends of the earth with the good news of Jesus. Praise God for their faithfulness!

Here, in this hymn of praise written 3000 years ago, the core theme of God's love for the whole world is celebrated in words of worship. The earnest request for God's blessing is a prayer with a purpose, that, as God's blessing is seen, it will be a witness to his goodness and lead to salvation.

In this psalm, God's blessings are seen as fairness and justice ('you rule the peoples with equity', v. 4), guidance and provision ('the land yields its harvest', v. 6). I hope that if you get the opportunity in church today, you will readily be able to name a blessing received from God in the past week!

Prayer

May the peoples praise you, God; may all the peoples praise you.

STEPHEN RAND

A kingdom of priests

Then Moses went up to God, and the Lord called to him from the mountain and said, 'This is what you are to say to the descendants of Jacob and what you are to tell the people of Israel: "You yourselves have seen what I did to Egypt, and how I carried you on eagles' wings and brought you to myself. Now if you obey me fully and keep my covenant, then out of all nations you will be my treasured possession. Although the whole earth is mine, you will be for me a kingdom of priests and a holy nation."'

Time has passed. God's mission to the nations had hung by a thread when it seemed that Abraham and Sarah were too old to have a child, but Isaac, the miracle baby, was born and Abraham's family became a great nation.

So, when the promise made to Abraham is repeated to Moses, it is no longer personal: Moses is to speak God's covenant to the whole people of Israel. Now it is a nation that carries the promise of blessing to all the nations. The promise comes with not so much small print as the biggest possible print condition of all: 'if you obey me fully... you will be my treasured possession.' Its role is to be 'a kingdom of priests and a holy nation'. Priests bring God to the people and the people to God. The people of Israel were to bring God to the whole world and the whole world to God. They were to be effective as priests, they were to be holy, demonstrating to the world how to live for God.

The apostle Peter explicitly restates this role to the church: 'But you are a chosen people, a royal priesthood, a holy nation, a people belonging to God... now you are the people of God... Live such good lives among the pagans that... they may see your good deeds and glorify God' (1 Peter 2:9–12). It's a reminder of a simple truth: if we are to *make* disciples we have to *be* disciples. We must 'walk the talk'.

Prayer

Loving Father, grant me your Spirit so that I may live my life in a way that encourages people to want to follow you. Amen

Stephen Rand

A house of prayer for all nations

'And foreigners who bind themselves to the Lord to minister to him, to love the name of the Lord, and to be his servants, all who keep the Sabbath without desecrating it and who hold fast to my covenant—these I will bring to my holy mountain and give them joy in my house of prayer. Their burnt offerings and sacrifices will be accepted on my altar; for my house will be called a house of prayer for all nations.'

Yesterday we saw that the people of Israel were called to be priests to the nations; today Isaiah emphasises that God's intention is for all nations to have access to his presence. The temple in Jerusalem is not an exclusive religious building dedicated to a local deity; it is open to all to meet the God of the universe. So foreigners (Gentiles) had a special dedicated area inside the temple. They couldn't get as close, in one sense, as the Jewish people, but they could get in.

Many commentators are convinced that when Jesus cleansed the temple (Mark 11:15–17) it was not only because commercial exploitation had sullied God's holy place but also because it was taking place in the temple courts, squeezing out the space reserved for the outsiders, the foreigners. As the tables go flying, it is this verse from Isaiah that he yells at the astonished traders.

Perhaps these were the same verses that the Ethiopian eunuch travelling home from Jerusalem was reading (Acts 8:26–40). Isaiah 56:3 would certainly have caught his eye: 'Let no foreigner who has bound himself to the Lord say, "The Lord will surely exclude me from his people." And let not any eunuch complain, "I am only a dry tree."' He would also have read on to discover that he was fully included in God's promise. No wonder he wanted to quiz Philip!

This is God's heart revealed. Jesus is for everyone; no one is to be excluded and everyone is granted the opportunity, by faith, to become part of his family.

Reflection

Is your home or church a 'house of prayer for all nations'? Is everyone welcome, regardless of their origin? Do your prayers have a global focus?

STEPHEN RAND

A vision for the nations

In the last days the mountain of the Lord's temple will be established as the highest of the mountains; it will be exalted above the hills, and peoples will stream to it. Many nations will come and say, 'Come, let us go up to the mountain of the Lord, to the temple of the God of Jacob. He will teach us his ways, so that we may walk in his paths.' The law will go out from Zion, the word of the Lord from Jerusalem. He will judge between many peoples and will settle disputes for strong nations far and wide. They will beat their swords into plough-shares and their spears into pruning hooks. Nation will not take up sword against nation, nor will they train for war any more.

How do you react to this passage? Do you find it full of hope, an inspiration for the future or feel it is unrealistic, misplaced optimism? I am fascinated that Micah and Isaiah (who has an almost identical prophecy in Isaiah 2:2–5) lifted their eyes above the immediate challenges facing the people of God and highlighted God's heart and plan for all the nations. Even more fascinating, it is a plan rooted in making disciples!

The temple—the place where God dwells—will draw people to come looking for teaching with the intention of living it out ('so that we may walk in his paths', v. 2). It is hard to imagine a better definition of a disciple.

Even better, see what impact this will have. Peace will break out—weapons of war will become tools of fruitfulness. This is yet another articulation of God's purpose in his mission to the nations, to restore *shalom*—the positive peacefulness that he always intended for human beings and his whole creation.

Reflection

Recently I was invited to 10 Downing Street for an Easter reception, where David Cameron described the UK as a 'Christian country'. Yet, in a time of austerity and recession, we still spend billions on weapons of war. You may think that both his statement and the military expenditure are justified, but undoubtedly the combination of the two has a negative impact on the mission of the Church for millions of people.

STEPHEN RAND

Incarnation: we have seen his glory

He came to that which was his own, but his own did not receive him. Yet to all who did receive him, to those who believed in his name, he gave the right to become children of God—children born not of natural descent, nor of human decision or a husband's will, but born of God. The Word became flesh and made his dwelling among us. We have seen his glory, the glory of the one and only Son, who came from the Father, full of grace and truth.

'For God so loved the world… ' that he did not send a message, but a messenger; he did not send a final demand, but the offer of a new start; he did not set up a religious institution or build a temple, but began a family. The way God does things is always significant: his method is a model for us to follow. Some of the greatest breakthroughs in mission have come when people have immersed themselves in the daily lives of those they want to reach for Christ.

In his Gospel, John uses the word 'glory' in relation to the cross of Jesus, the faithful obedience of the Son to his Father that led to his death; his incarnation fulfilled and complete. In 2013, the Word still has to become flesh in the lives of those who have been 'born of God'. The mission of God still demands incarnation, life and love expressed in the daily reality of home, family, work, school, leisure, community.

'In your lives you must think and act like Christ Jesus,' says Paul (Philippians 2:5–8, New Century Version). 'Christ himself was like God in everything. But he did not think that being equal with God was something to be used for his own benefit. But he gave up his place with God and made himself nothing. He was born as a man and became like a servant. And when he was living as a man, he humbled himself and was fully obedient to God, even when that caused his death—death on a cross.'

Prayer

Lord, grant me the humility, the obedience and the commitment to live for you day by day. Amen

STEPHEN RAND

The hope of nations

This was to fulfil what was spoken through the prophet Isaiah: 'Here is my servant whom I have chosen, the one I love, in whom I delight; I will put my Spirit on him, and he will proclaim justice to the nations. He will not quarrel or cry out; no one will hear his voice in the streets. A bruised reed he will not break, and a smouldering wick he will not snuff out, till he has brought justice through to victory. In his name the nations will put their hope.'

What prompted Matthew to insert this long quotation from Isaiah (42:1–4) into his Gospel? Immediately before this, he explained that the Pharisees were plotting to kill Jesus. Jesus withdraws, only to be followed by large crowds seeking healing. He heals many, but urges them to tell no one. It seems that Matthew is concerned to balance two realities that seem contradictory, but reflect very clearly that God's ways are not our ways. Jesus' healing ministry reveals him to be the Messiah—'my servant whom I have chosen'—but he does not return hatred with force. Instead, his ministry is characterised by humility, by gentleness—but not by weakness.

Perhaps Matthew is also prompted to remind his readers, both Jewish and Gentile, that the suffering servant predicted by Isaiah had a ministry for all the nations. He would bring them judgment (justice); he would also bring them hope. In fact, it is because he is the suffering servant that he also is the only one who can bring them hope. The phrase 'In his name' (v. 21) is a reminder that when Peter stood before the Sanhedrin, he told the Jewish leaders, 'Salvation is found in no one else, for there is no other name under heaven by which we must be saved' (Acts 4:12).

The fact that Jesus is *the* way (not one way of many) is at the heart of the mission imperative. On the one hand, the gospel is inclusive—it is for all—but, on the other, it is exclusive: Jesus is the only way. It is this combination that gives hope to the nations.

Prayer

May my life be characterised by the humility and gentleness that brings hope to the vulnerable and the broken.

STEPHEN RAND

Fishing for disciples

As Jesus was walking beside the Sea of Galilee, he saw two brothers, Simon called Peter and his brother Andrew. They were casting a net into the lake, for they were fishermen. 'Come, follow me,' Jesus said, 'and I will send you out to fish for people.' At once they left their nets and followed him. Going on from there, he saw two other brothers, James son of Zebedee and his brother John. They were in a boat with their father Zebedee, preparing their nets. Jesus called them, and immediately they left the boat and their father and followed him.

This was the day when their lives changed for ever. One moment they were about their daily routine; the next they were walking alongside an itinerant teacher, not knowing where they were going, what adventures they would have on the way, nor even where it would end.

We have seen that God's heart, from the beginning, has been for people of all nations. Now let us think about what it means to be a disciple. There are some obvious clues in today's reading. It begins with a call from Jesus to 'follow me' (v. 19). That call is not dependent on position, intellect or learning—these four were fishermen. They did not have to be special or clever, just willing to follow. They were not asked to sign a form, pass an exam, learn a catechism. It was an active, ongoing response, not a one-off decision. It required commitment. It was instant ('immediately', v. 22), and it was total ('they left the boat and their father', v. 22).

There was a purpose, too: they would be 'sent out' (v. 19). I did Latin at school—actually, Latin did me—and the first verb I learned was *mitto*, to send, which is the origin of the word 'mission'. So often we do mission by inviting people in, but God is a sending God and the disciples were to be sent out to 'fish for people' (v. 19). They knew that fishing was hard work, sometimes dangerous, and the results were not always guaranteed. One thing, however, would change: their new kind of fishing would not be bad for the fish and only good for the fishermen.

Prayer

Help me to be ready to respond to your call and follow you.

Stephen Rand

Each one heard

When the day of Pentecost came, they were all together in one place... All of them were filled with the Holy Spirit and began to speak in other tongues as the Spirit enabled them. Now there were staying in Jerusalem God-fearing Jews from every nation under heaven. When they heard this sound, a crowd came together in bewilderment, because each one heard their own language being spoken. Utterly amazed, they asked: 'Aren't all these who are speaking Galileans? Then how is it that each of us hears them in our native language?'... Then Peter... addressed the crowd: '... This is what was spoken by the prophet Joel: "In the last days, God says, I will pour out my Spirit on all people."'

The birthday of the Church... and what a party! Some even thought the disciples were drunk, the atmosphere was so intoxicating. Amid the confusion and clamour, something remarkable was happening. At the tower of Babel, the multitude of languages had brought confusion and division but, at Pentecost, God's Spirit enabled everyone to hear in their own language and come together in God's family, the Church.

Pentecost is a reminder that God's purposes will not be thwarted by human sin. He *will* build his Church. He *will* enable people to hear in their own language. He *will* make disciples of all nations. He *will* welcome you to play your part in his great plan of salvation. On that day of Pentecost, the Church grew from a few hundred to a few thousand. Now, perhaps two billion people describe themselves as Christians. One reason for this remarkable phenomenon is that some Christians were prepared to risk everything for the sake of telling others about Jesus. They explored unknown areas of the world. They translated the Bible, built hospitals, established schools, planted churches. They were determined to play their part in making disciples of all nations.

Today, people from across the world flock to the UK, just as they did to Jerusalem. Pray that the church will be alert and respond to the opportunities this offers.

Prayer

Lord Jesus, pour out your Spirit on all people.

STEPHEN RAND

Learning to be salt and light

Now when Jesus saw the crowds, he went up on a mountainside and sat down. His disciples came to him, and he began to teach them... 'You are the salt of the earth. But if the salt loses its saltiness, how can it be made salty again? It is no longer good for anything, except to be thrown out and trampled underfoot. You are the light of the world.'

Disciples are followers; disciples are learners. The Sermon on the Mount is firmly set in the traditional model of the rabbi and his disciples, the teacher sitting and delivering wisdom to his followers. Jesus, however, was no ordinary teacher. His listeners were amazed by the sermon, 'because he taught as one who had authority' (Matthew 7:29). Mahatma Gandhi said, 'If then I had to face only the Sermon on the Mount and my own interpretation of it, I should not hesitate to say, "Oh, yes, I am a Christian."'

The passage highlights two aspects of what it means to be a disciple of Jesus. Salt is a preservative that stops things going bad and it also gives flavour. There is an additional modern meaning: it helps you grip when the road gets treacherous. The comparison with salt and light carries real encouragement as a little can go such a long way. It does not take many dedicated followers of Jesus to have a significant impact on local and national communities.

Light, too, is a positive and sought-after commodity. Disciples are to bring light to the world: 'Let your light shine before others, that they may see your good deeds and glorify your Father in heaven' (Matthew 5:16). Here is that emphasis again on disciples living out what they learn.

That was where Gandhi stumbled. He thought that what passed as Christianity was a negation of the Sermon on the Mount: 'I like your Christ, I do not like your Christians. Your Christians are so unlike your Christ.' In a sense he was passing judgment on the same basis that Jesus himself did: 'By this everyone will know that you are my disciples, if you love one another' (John 13:35).

Prayer

Help me day-by-day to learn from you and be salt and light for you.

STEPHEN RAND

Workers in the harvest field

Jesus went through all the towns and villages, teaching in their synagogues, proclaiming the good news of the kingdom and healing every disease and illness. When he saw the crowds, he had compassion on them, because they were harassed and helpless, like sheep without a shepherd. Then he said to his disciples, 'The harvest is plentiful but the workers are few. Ask the Lord of the harvest, therefore, to send out workers into his harvest field.' Jesus called his twelve disciples to him and gave them authority to drive out impure spirits and to heal every disease and illness.

Matthew sums up Jesus' holistic ministry: it involves teaching (focused on the mind, for understanding), preaching (focused on the spirit, for a response to God) and healing (focused on the body, for wholeness). Authentic Christian ministry will always have this breadth of concern and will always be motivated by compassion. Mission—making disciples—is not about counting numbers; it is about sharing God's love.

True compassion is not just an emotion; it will always lead to action. In the New Testament, this word is used only of Jesus and, whenever he has compassion, he acts—touching the skin of the person with leprosy, the eyes of the blind—and this makes a difference, bringing healing.

Today's passage is the exception. Jesus does not act; instead, he invites his disciples to pray for workers in the harvest field. Then he immediately commissions the Twelve and gives them his authority to become workers, to do the same miracles he has been doing—restoring, healing, making whole. The disciples are followers, they are learners… and they are workers. Some are sent by the Spirit of God to other countries, but geography is not the main factor. Every disciple is sent into their own street, their own town, to be a worker for God's kingdom.

I once met a woman who realised that whenever the TV news showed a disaster, Christians would be working to bring help. So she would switch off the TV… and pray. That was how she became a worker in God's harvest field.

Prayer
Lord, fill me with your compassion and stir me into action.

STEPHEN RAND

Receive the Holy Spirit

On the evening of that first day of the week, when the disciples were together, with the doors locked for fear of the Jewish leaders, Jesus came and stood among them and said, 'Peace be with you!' After he said this, he showed them his hands and side. The disciples were overjoyed when they saw the Lord. Again Jesus said, 'Peace be with you! As the Father has sent me, I am sending you.' And with that he breathed on them and said, 'Receive the Holy Spirit.'

Here is the story of the disciples getting involved in mission.

Step 1: Fear: Who could blame them for locking the door? Jesus had just been executed; they might be next. Our lives might not be under threat, but when we face up to the challenge of being a disciple-making disciple, then our way of life may well be under threat. Stepping out of our comfort zone may well cause fear.

Step 2: The presence of Jesus: You cannot lock any doors that will keep Jesus out.

Step 3: Peace: When Jesus comes, and we know his presence, he brings peace. He shows them his hands and his side—he has paid the price so that we might know his presence and his peace.

Step 4: Joy: What a turnaround! One moment they were full of fear; now they are full of joy. Jesus makes all the difference. One of the greatest breakthroughs for individual Christians is when we discover the joy of serving God.

Step 5: Sent: 'As the Father has sent me, I am sending you' (v. 21). The mission of Jesus is the mission of his disciples.

Step 6: Receive: Step 5 might send me spiralling back to the beginning, the doors locked, full of fear once again. However, just as the presence of Jesus changed that, even as he gives them the task, he promises that his presence will remain, through the gift of his Spirit.

It is that same gift, the same Spirit, he promises to all his disciples.

Reflection

When God calls, he equips. We are promised the resources we need to be disciples because we are promised his Spirit.

STEPHEN RAND

The great commission

> Then the eleven disciples went to Galilee, to the mountain where Jesus had told them to go. When they saw him, they worshipped him; but some doubted. Then Jesus came to them and said, 'All authority in heaven and on earth has been given to me. Therefore go and make disciples of all nations, baptising them in the name of the Father and of the Son and of the Holy Spirit, and teaching them to obey everything I have commanded you. And surely I am with you always, to the very end of the age.'

This call to mission is a parallel to the one we read yesterday. In the locked upper room he had shown them the marks of his suffering. That suffering is, in one sense, the sign and source of the authority he claims here. The suffering servant is the king of all creation: he has authority. *'Therefore* go…' (v. 19): the task of mission stems from that authority. We do not make disciples because it seems like a good idea; we have been commanded to go into the world by the one who died for the world.

We go with the same mission. The main action described in the sentence is 'make disciples' (v. 19): the going, baptising and teaching are all aspects of what needs to be done in order to make disciples. We have to go (not wait for them to come to us). We baptise to demonstrate that disciples make a new start and belong to a new family and we pass on the teaching of Jesus. The learners then become the teachers of the next generation of learners and that is how God builds his Church.

I am encouraged to see churches grappling with what it means to make disciples rather than simply encourage people to come to church. I am excited by new expressions of church that put the emphasis on reaching out to those who do not know Jesus rather than making the faithful comfortable!

Jesus completes his commission with the promise of his presence: 'I am with you always' (v. 20). This is the promise fulfilled by the gift of the Holy Spirit. You are not alone.

Prayer
Gracious Master, help me to be a true disciple, engaged in helping others to become disciples. Amen

STEPHEN RAND

Bible stories rediscovered: Samson

'When God wants to do something special, he has a baby'; so I heard recently. The speaker went on to mention three people: Moses, Samson and Jesus. Moses led his people from slavery to the promised land, Jesus—well, he hardly needs explaining, but Samson? His adventures are well known: he killed a lion and told a riddle about honey, he killed 1000 Philistines with the jawbone of a donkey, he set fire to wheat fields by putting torches in the tails of 150 pairs of foxes. He is also remembered for his weakness for women—most memorably Delilah, who has been much depicted in art. It's an exciting story, with 'superman' aspects, but is there more to it than that?

Samson's story is not in the lectionary used by many churches, so it does not often appear in public reading or preaching and we may not have thought much about him since Sunday school days. We may now find that it raises difficult questions: did God sanction all that killing (including the mistreatment of 300 foxes)? Does the Bible really portray women like Delilah as beautiful temptresses?

If God did want to do something special, we may wonder what went wrong. Over the next eleven days, we will be taking a fresh look at Samson, who is found in the book of Judges, at a time when Israel's situation was dire. God's people were drifting further and further away from him; a rescuer was needed. Cue Samson—a man set aside for God and with much potential, but also serious weaknesses.

Samson has been considered a 'type' of Christ, which may seem mystifying, but what we find is that, despite all his failings, the Spirit of God was at work in him. Samson often seems to have forgotten about God, but God did not forget about Samson. As we approach the events of his life, we need to do so attentively. His story is much more complex than we might think and full of surprises. It is shocking, but also profoundly human. It reminds us that even in a nation far from God, led by a flawed, fallible specimen of humanity, God is in control and his plans go on.

Rosie Ward

Great expectations

Again the Israelites did evil in the eyes of the Lord, so the Lord delivered them into the hands of the Philistines for forty years. A certain man of Zorah, named Manoah, from the clan of the Danites, had a wife who was childless, unable to give birth. The angel of the Lord appeared to her and said, 'You are barren and childless, but you are going to become pregnant and give birth to a son.'

The story starts with a reminder, which echoes through the pages of the book of Judges, that Israel 'did evil in the eyes of the Lord' (v. 1) and then God handed them over to their enemies. Earlier in Judges, the pattern of rebellion and retribution is followed by repentance, rescue and restoration: the land ends up at peace. This time, though, there is no cry of misery, let alone penitence, and no rest. Verse 1 is intended to warn us that Israel is really in trouble, its society falling apart; this will not be a happy story.

Who were the Philistines? You may recall them from the story of David and Goliath (1 Samuel 17). They were an aggressive nation, established on the coastal plain between Egypt and Gaza, constantly pressing inland into the land occupied by the Israelites. A few chapters earlier in Judges we are told that the Israelites had abandoned the Lord and were worshipping a variety of foreign gods, including the gods of the Philistines.

The context is not promising, but God is there. Immediately we are into a story full of promise as God appears in angelic form to announce a birth to a barren woman. It is a while since Christmas and the words of Gabriel to Mary, but these verses bring them to mind, along with the other miraculous births foretold to Sarah, Rachel, Hannah and Elizabeth. God's plan, as so often, involves the most unlikely people—in this case, Manoah and his wife (who is never named).

His people may not have cried out to him, but God has taken the initiative nevertheless. Grace abounds to his hapless people.

Reflection
God so often brings new hope in difficult situations.

ROSIE WARD

A Nazirite

Then the woman went to her husband and told him, 'A man of God came to me. He looked like an angel of God, very awesome. I didn't ask him where he came from, and he didn't tell me his name. But he said to me, "You will become pregnant and have a son. Now then, drink no wine or other fermented drink and do not eat anything unclean, because the boy will be a Nazirite of God from the womb until the day of his death."'

The boy is to be a Nazirite. This commitment is described in Numbers 6 and involved not drinking wine, not touching or going near a dead body and keeping hair long, not cutting or shaving it. It was normally undertaken voluntarily and temporarily, but Samson was to be a Nazirite for life. All three aspects of the vow are important in the narrative: Samson kills a lion in a vineyard, returns to the carcass and makes up a riddle about it; and Delilah finds that the secret of his strength is his uncut hair.

Here, we notice that Samson's mother may have been chosen for her great faith. She seems more astute than her husband, and, like Mary, she takes the angel at his word. She is convinced she has seen an angel and, since angels do not lie, she must be about to have a baby. A few verses later, when Manoah is worried that they will die because they have seen God, she is quick to allay his fears.

We then learn that the boy is born and named Samson: 'the Lord blessed him, and the Spirit of the Lord began to stir him' (vv. 24–25). In Luke 2:40 we read similar words about Jesus, that he 'grew and became strong; he was filled with wisdom, and the grace of God was on him'. The Israelites are in a parlous state and God has gone to great lengths to prepare someone to lead them. Samson is a boy with promise and, most significantly, the Spirit of the Lord is on him—something we will see repeated many times through these chapters.

Prayer

Lord, please fill me with your Spirit today. Amen

ROSIE WARD

Down to Philistine country

Samson went down to Timnah and saw there a young Philistine woman. When he returned, he said to his father and mother, 'I have seen a Philistine woman in Timnah; now get her for me as my wife.' His father and mother replied, 'Isn't there an acceptable woman among your relatives or among all our people? Must you go to the uncircumcised Philistines to get a wife?' But Samson said to his father, 'Get her for me. She's the right one for me.' (His parents did not know that this was from the Lord, who was seeking an occasion to confront the Philistines; for at that time they were ruling over Israel.)

Yesterday we read of Samson's great potential. Today he does not look so promising. We are introduced to two important strands of the story: Samson and women, and the Philistines. The first thing on Samson's agenda seems to be finding a wife, but, if he is a Nazirite, devoted to the Lord, and called to be Israel's judge, surely his primary responsibility is the people of Israel? Even if he were just a God-fearing Israelite, he would not have dreamt of visiting Philistine country, still less of marrying a Philistine woman. Israel has already sold out to the values of the Philistine world, and so has Samson—the man called to rescue his nation.

We may well have every sympathy with Samson's parents at the behaviour of their headstrong son. Parents then and now want the best for their children, so their comment has a modern ring about it, but there is a twist in the tale. Just as we find ourselves agreeing with them, we come to the section in brackets. Why would the Lord be prompting Samson to do this? It is surprising to find that this is all part of God's plan, but it is important for the rest of the story. God needed Samson to pick a fight with the Philistines. It seems that for God's people to overcome the Philistines, they must fight them, not be friendly neighbours. So, God uses the frailties of his people, and the enemies of Israel, for his ultimate purposes.

Reflection
'"My thoughts are not your thoughts…" declares the Lord' (Isaiah 55:8).

ROSIE WARD

The Spirit of the Lord

Samson went down to Timnah together with his father and mother. As they approached the vineyards of Timnah, suddenly a young lion came roaring towards him. The Spirit of the Lord came powerfully upon him so that he tore the lion apart with his bare hands as he might have torn a young goat. But he told neither his father nor his mother what he had done. Then he went down and talked with the woman, and he liked her.

Thus Samson goes with his parents into Philistine territory. We might ask why he was going towards vineyards when his vow forbade him from drinking products made from grapes. Even if he is in the wrong place, though, in some way we cannot quite grasp, God is with him (v. 4). So it is that Samson is in the wrong place, but also the right place.

Then he kills a lion. According to his Nazirite vow, we would expect him to have thought, 'A dead lion is a carcass and I am not supposed to go near one of those.' If Nazirites accidentally had contact with someone who had died, there was provision for them to reconsecrate themselves to God. For Samson deliberately to put himself in a position where he creates a carcass seems to fly in the face of his vow. Yet, God is in this—Samson killed the lion because the 'Spirit of the Lord' was upon him. This is more and more puzzling. It is far more than a straight case of disobedience.

We also read that his parents did not know what he had done. How that could be is not clear, but the information does seem to be significant. All through the story we are told about what people know or do not know. Here again, it seems, Samson does not know what his true role should be, that he should not be fraternising with the Philistines and he should certainly not be thinking of marrying one.

In God's economy the events are unfolding. It seems that Samson is already way off track, yet God is unmistakably with him, empowering him to act.

Prayer

Lead us not into temptation; but deliver us from evil.

ROSIE WARD

The riddle

Some time later, when he went back to marry her, he turned aside to look at the lion's carcass, and in it he saw a swarm of bees and some honey. He scooped out the honey with his hands and ate as he went along. When he rejoined his parents, he gave them some, and they too ate it. But he did not tell them that he had taken the honey from the lion's carcass. Now his father went down to see the woman. And there Samson held a feast... 'Let me tell you a riddle,' Samson said... 'Out of the eater, something to eat; out of the strong, something sweet.'

Samson's vow forbade him from approaching a carcass, but, as he passed the dead lion, he 'turned aside' not just to look but also to touch and scoop out the honey. Did he think about his vow? If he did, perhaps it was his guilt that led him to not tell his parents. We may feel that would have made his guilt likely to be even greater, but, before we judge him, we have to look at ourselves. How easy it can be to rationalise our actions when our conscience pricks us!

So it is that we then come to one of the most well-known parts of the story—the riddle. Riddles are popular in every culture and there are some ancient parallels to Samson's impossible riddle. It was intended to keep the guests puzzling through the seven days of the feast. Samson may have thought he had confounded them, but, just before the deadline, the answer comes back: 'What is sweeter than honey? What is stronger than a lion?' (v. 18).

Samson is angry: his wife has wheedled the answer out of him and has betrayed him—a hint of what is to come. Thus, the men of the town are able to win the rash wager he made. He now owes them 30 linen garments and 30 sets of clothes. The story goes on to tell how the Spirit comes on Samson and, to get the clothes, he goes to a Philistine city, kills 30 men and distributes their clothes to fulfil his promise.

Is Samson a saviour or a self-indulgent sinner?

Prayer

Lord, you have given me so much. Help me to be true to you. Amen

ROSIE WARD

Why the violence?

Samson said to [his father-in-law], 'This time I have a right to get even with the Philistines; I will really harm them.' So he went out and caught three hundred foxes and tied them tail to tail in pairs. He then fastened a torch to every pair of tails, lit the torches and let the foxes loose in the standing corn of the Philistines. He burned up the shocks and standing grain, together with the vineyards and olive groves. When the Philistines asked, 'Who did this?' they were told, 'Samson, the Timnite's son-in-law, because his wife was given to his companion.' So the Philistines went up and burned her and her father to death. Samson said to them, 'Since you've acted like this, I swear that I won't stop until I get my revenge on you.' He attacked them viciously and slaughtered many of them.

What are we to make of the violence of the Old Testament? Here we have Samson out for revenge. To 'get even' with the Philistines he kills (or at least, injures) 300 foxes without a thought, the Philistines burn his wife and her father to death and, in return, he slaughters many Philistines.

We have a choice: we can ignore the Old Testament, we can explain away the violence or we can see it as God's way, then, of dealing with the other nations. Perhaps part of the answer lies in these verses themselves. While Samson is violent, so are the Philistines. We may see his violence as inexcusable, but, by the standards of the time, it is 'normal' and the actions of God's people, unlike those of their enemies, are moderated by a God who commanded that human life be respected.

God wanted the nations around Israel destroyed because of their evil. Their religions involved the worship of idols and human sacrifices. He wanted to keep his people pure and keeping them separate was the only way to do this. Under a very different covenant, we do not take up arms against other nations or religions; our struggle is against 'principalities and powers'.

Reflection

How do I answer the charge that God is an ethnic cleanser?

ROSIE WARD

Betrayal

Then three thousand men from Judah went down to the cave in the rock of Etam and said to Samson, 'Don't you realise that the Philistines are rulers over us? What have you done to us?' He answered, 'I merely did to them what they did to me.' They said to him, 'We've come to tie you up and hand you over to the Philistines.' Samson said, 'Swear to me that you won't kill me yourselves.' 'Agreed,' they answered. 'We will only tie you up and hand you over to them. We will not kill you.' So they bound him with two new ropes and led him up from the rock. As he approached Lehi, the Philistines came towards him shouting. The Spirit of the Lord came powerfully upon him. The ropes on his arms became like charred flax, and the bindings dropped from his hands. Finding a fresh jawbone of a donkey, he grabbed it and struck down a thousand men.

Today we go from one slaughter of Philistines to another. After Samson takes brutal revenge for the killing of his wife and father-in-law, he takes refuge in a cave (v. 8). Behaviour any less like that of a judge of Israel would be hard to imagine, but it is to this place that representatives of both nations come. Ironically, they come to him not in his capacity as judge, but to sort out the mess he has created.

The Philistines come to take their revenge on Samson, to take him prisoner (v. 9). So some men from Judah decide it would be better to hand Samson over than risk them attacking the whole nation. God's Spirit is with him still, though, and, in a show of strength, he breaks the ropes, seizes a jawbone (from another carcass) and strikes down 1000 men.

Here we see Samson the human failure. He cannot control himself. His anger is eagerly aroused and he acts on it, unable to understand that it is possible to control anger. In today's culture, 'self-expression' is the order of the day, but we can see what damage it can do and the greater the position of influence, the greater the potential to damage others.

Reflection

'In your anger do not sin' (Ephesians 4:26).

ROSIE WARD

God provides

Because he was very thirsty, [Samson] cried out to the Lord, 'You have given your servant this great victory. Must I now die of thirst and fall into the hands of the uncircumcised?' Then God opened up the hollow place in Lehi, and water came out of it. When Samson drank, his strength returned and he revived. So the spring was called En Hakkore, and it is still there in Lehi. Samson led Israel for twenty years in the days of the Philistines.

What image of Samson comes to mind after a week of readings? Comic Superman, freedom fighter—or human failure? Perhaps there is an element of all these in his story. Here, at the end of chapter 15, we may find Samson a more sympathetic figure as, alone and thirsty, he cries out to God.

As we note Samson's aloneness, it is worth reflecting on another reason for his failure. Moses was encouraged to share the load of judging with others (Exodus 18:13–26), but Samson shares the task with no one else. He never asks for advice, but acts alone—a rugged individualist. On our own we are more fallible, which is why God calls us to community. Individualists, people who will not take advice from others or believe they have a hotline to God, can wreck churches.

This is perhaps the first time that Samson cannot cope, but, even if he has no one with him at this low point, at least he has God. He has not said a word to God in chapters 14 or 15. Now he is at the end of his resources and, although his prayer is only about his own needs, God answers and gives water, just as he has done for his people so many times before. Amazingly, God stays with him. It is a reminder that God stays with us longer than we stay with God.

In the final verse, we have the narrator's summary, repeated in 16:31, that Samson led Israel for 20 years. Are we meant to applaud as we approach the climax of the story?

Reflection

How willing am I to ask others for help? How much do I really depend on God?

ROSIE WARD

A fatal attraction

Some time later, he fell in love with a woman in the Valley of Sorek whose name was Delilah. The rulers of the Philistines went to her and said, 'See if you can lure him into showing you the secret of his great strength and how we can overpower him so we may tie him up and subdue him. Each one of us will give you eleven hundred shekels of silver.' So Delilah said to Samson, 'Tell me the secret of your great strength and how you can be tied up and subdued.' Samson answered her, 'If anyone ties me with seven fresh bowstrings that have not been dried, I'll become as weak as any other man.'

The name 'Delilah' has become synonymous with fatal infatuation. Delilah has been much celebrated in music, film and art, often providing the excuse for a nude. She has been viewed as a temptress and somehow typical of women, in a way we might question. The real Delilah was more a pawn in a game, which is played out in chapter 16—the final drama in the Samson story.

Samson is in Gaza, a Philistine city about 25 miles away from Zorah, where he grew up. Gaza was also the headquarters of the Philistines. It was where they had the temple to Dagon—the god they worshipped. So, we might ask ourselves why was Samson there, seemingly in the wrong place at the wrong time? In God's economy, however, Samson will need to be in Philistine territory if he is to defeat the Philistines. So, while we may continue to puzzle about Samson's actions and choices, if God is in control, then we can only marvel at how God uses this errant human judge to bring about his purposes.

We know Samson's weakness for women; it has got him into trouble already and, here, the Philistines use it against him. We are not told that Delilah was a Philistine, but she probably was. At least she has a name, unlike Samson's mother and his other women, but Samson's love for her proves fatal…

Prayer

Thank you that you use us, even in our weaknesses, for your purposes.

ROSIE WARD

Eyeless in Gaza

After putting [Samson] to sleep on her lap, [Delilah] called for someone to shave off the seven braids of his hair, and so began to subdue him. And his strength left him. Then she called, 'Samson, the Philistines are upon you!' He awoke from his sleep and thought, 'I'll go out as before and shake myself free.' But he did not know that the Lord had left him. Then the Philistines seized him, gouged out his eyes and took him down to Gaza. Binding him with bronze shackles, they set him to grinding corn in the prison.

The Philistines have bribed Delilah to find the secret of Samson's strength, but Samson values his vow more than they may have bargained for and, at first, he gives her spurious answers (vv. 6–16). Three times he easily escapes Philistine captivity. Then he tells her about the Nazirite vow: 'If my head were shaved, my strength would leave me' (v. 17). So it is that we come to the verses in today's passage.

Samson is shaved and his strength is gone. The words in verse 20, 'But he did not know that the Lord had left him', must be some of the saddest words in the Bible. He is taken by his enemies and treated as an animal by those from whom he was supposed to rescue God's people.

These same words have been written of many Christian organisations and individuals, too. It is all too easy for us to think that our effectiveness or the effectiveness of the Church is in itself, but the Lord will not give his glory to another; he will not allow us to think that spiritual power comes from us.

Samson has given in yet again to his weakness for women. The original readers would have made the connection between one man's relationship with a woman and Israel's relationship with seductive neighbours. For us, it may not be other nations who are pulling us away from God, but other sins. This may be a stark reminder that the sins we fail to deal with may be our downfall or at least may damage us.

Prayer

Lord Jesus, help me to be alert to anything that draws me away from you.
Amen

ROSIE WARD

'Do you remember me?'

Then Samson prayed to the Lord, 'O Sovereign Lord, remember me. O God, please strengthen me just once more, and let me with one blow get revenge on the Philistines for my two eyes.' Then Samson reached towards the two central pillars on which the temple stood. Bracing himself against them, his right hand on the one and his left hand on the other, Samson said, 'Let me die with the Philistines!' Then he pushed with all his might, and down came the temple on the rulers and all the people in it. Thus he killed many more when he died than while he lived.

Imprisoned in Gaza, Samson was set to grind corn, which was women's work, intended to humiliate him. While he was in prison, however, his hair began to grow, setting the scene for the final denouement. The Philistines celebrate their victory and call Samson out to perform for them.

The final 'not knowing' is what the Philistines did not know. Samson's vow may have been broken, but his hair was growing again and his God is the God of grace abounding, the God who does the unexpected. Ironically, it is in a hostile place of worship that Samson utters his first formal prayer to God. Apart from the verses we looked at on Friday, Samson has always relied on himself, but, at this point, he is out of his depth. He says, 'Remember me. O God, please…' (v. 28) and God's ear is open to his cry.

In this dramatic end to the story, the temple collapses and, with it, so does Samson. On the face of it we might see him as a suicide bomber, someone who realised that it is possible to kill a great number of people if you are willing to die with them. There is certainly ambiguity here, but I prefer to believe that, as all the way through Samson's life, the message is that the triumph is God's. However far away we are from God it is always possible to come back, as the prodigal son did. We believe in a God who believes in us far more strongly than we believe in him.

Prayer

Even if I forget you, Lord, do not forget me.

ROSIE WARD

'I call you friends'

Friends are easy to come by nowadays. If you belong to Facebook (and a high proportion of people of all ages do), you can make a new 'friend' with the click of a mouse. Then, if you fall out with them, you can 'unfriend' (such a horrible word) them with another click.

Many Facebook members have several hundred 'friends'. I wonder how possible it is to be a real friend to so many people. Certainly, in the ancient world—the world that shaped Jesus' experience of friendship—it would have seemed unreal as friendship was closely connected with love. The Greek word for 'friend', *philos* comes from one of the common Greek verbs for 'love', *phileo*. A friend was one who loved and who loved to the point of being willing to give his or her life for a friend.

Another important aspect of friendship in Jesus' world was that of frankness. Many relationships were based on expediency, power imbalances, what each could obtain from the other and, therefore, words were carefully measured and not necessarily frank. By contrast, friends were those who spoke openly and honestly to one another, not flattering each other, but telling the truth in love. This is only possible in a relationship between equals, which is another mark of friendship, then and now. Friends do not jockey for position or status; instead they want to be alongside one another, serving each other, as Jesus did when he washed his disciples' feet in John 13.

All this means that using the image of friendship to describe our relationship with God is particularly powerful and, perhaps, startling. How can we be in a relationship of equals with our Creator—the one who made our world and all that is in it, who sustains us in life? It is a good question. The answer is that it is only possible because Jesus made it so. He came into our lives and called us to be his friends, so we are friends of his Father, too.

Our human experiences of friendship can help us to learn how to be friends of God and some of the passages that follow are about this, but the call is always to go deeper, to grasp the unbelievable gift that is offered to us, which is to become true friends of God.

Helen Julian CSF

Friends for life

So [Naomi] said, 'See, your sister-in-law has gone back to her people and to her gods; return after your sister-in-law.' But Ruth said, 'Do not press me to leave you or to turn back from following you! Where you go, I will go; where you lodge, I will lodge; your people shall be my people, and your God my God. Where you die, I will die—there will I be buried. May the Lord do thus and so to me, and more as well, if even death parts me from you!' When Naomi saw that she was determined to go with her, she said no more to her.

Mothers-in-law do not usually get a very good press, but Naomi is different. She had gone with her husband away from Judah, to the land of Moab—away from Judah, because of a famine. Her husband had died in Moab; her two sons married local women, then both sons died, too. She is now planning to return to her own country. One daughter-in-law agrees to stay in Moab, but Ruth is determined to go with Naomi. Their relationship is such that she does not want for them to be parted, but to continue together, even though it means leaving her own country and going somewhere strange.

She is determined to embrace everything about Naomi's new life—the country, the people and even her God. Even in death she will not expect to return to her own land.

In this, Ruth is an image of God's own covenant faithfulness. God does not leave when the going gets tough. God's commitment to us is unconditional, as Ruth's is to Naomi. As a widow, her commitment to Naomi's family no longer has a hold on her, but she chooses it again.

This is a dramatic example, but any long-term friendship requires us to keep choosing to 'go with' our friend. It may not mean a physical journey, but one of remaining alongside through changes of thought and priority and life circumstances.

The story of Ruth and Naomi is a short one of just four chapters—why not read it all? Then you could reflect on your own experiences of long-term friendship.

Reflection
Where has faithful friendship taken you?

HELEN JULIAN CSF

A friend in need

Now when Job's three friends heard of all these troubles that had
come upon him, each of them set out from his home—Eliphaz the
Temanite, Bildad the Shuhite, and Zophar the Naamathite. They
met together to go and console and comfort him. When they saw
him from a distance, they did not recognise him, and they raised
their voices and wept aloud; they tore their robes and threw dust
in the air upon their heads. They sat with him on the ground seven
days and seven nights, and no one spoke a word to him, for they
saw that his suffering was very great.

Again a bit of back story is needed here. The book of Job recounts the
life of a virtuous man who gets caught up in a debate between God and
'the Accuser', or, Satan. Will he remain virtuous if all that he has is
taken away? First, all his possessions are stolen and his servants killed,
then his children die in a disaster. He still does not blame God, so, next,
he is afflicted with sores all over his body. This is the point at which
today's passage begins.

Job's friends arrive and they begin well. They act as mourners did at
that time, as the word translated as 'console' literally means to rock the
body, while sitting on the ground, which was the position mourners
adopted. They are simply alongside him in his great distress and they
do not try to say anything.

Sadly, however, this does not last and the next chapters are filled
with their attempts to find an explanation for Job's sufferings, to con-
vince him that somehow he has deserved what has happened to him,
God is justified. Job does not find this helpful: 'miserable comforters
are you all', he responds (16:2).

One of the hardest parts of friendship is being alongside a friend in
distress. It is natural to want to make some sense of it all, but that may
often be for our sake rather than our friend's. Sometimes the best thing
we can do is simply to sit alongside them, sharing their mourning.

Reflection

How easy do you find it simply to be with a friend in distress?

HELEN JULIAN CSF

Lover and friend

My beloved is all radiant and ruddy, distinguished among ten thousand. His head is the finest gold; his locks are wavy, black as a raven. His eyes are like doves beside springs of water, bathed in milk, fitly set. His cheeks are like beds of spices, yielding fragrance. His lips are lilies, distilling liquid myrrh. His arms are rounded gold, set with jewels. His body is ivory work, encrusted with sapphires... His speech is most sweet, and he is altogether desirable. This is my beloved and this is my friend, O daughters of Jerusalem.

I find it very touching to hear the widows of soldiers killed on active service say of them, as they frequently do, 'He was my best friend.' Along with the passion of sexual relationship, marriage, children, went friendship.

The Song of Solomon does not lack passion. Indeed, it has often been something of an embarrassment to biblical commentators, with its frank celebration of the body and the urgency of its desire. This passage is just one of many. In this case, it is in the voice of 'the Bride', praising the beauty of her beloved. She uses many images from the natural world, some of which are obvious, such as his raven black hair, while others are rather more obscure, such as the doves washing in milk. Commentators point out another level to such references, too—that many of the descriptions are reminiscent of language used elsewhere to describe the temple in Jerusalem, the city at the heart of Israel's faith.

This points to the two ways in which this book has been interpreted and it can speak to us of friendship. Along with the celebration of human passion, there has always been an interpretation of it as being about the love affair of God and the human soul and the Church, the Bride of Christ. So far, we have been looking at different dimensions of human friendship. Now, we also begin to consider the idea of friendship with God and him with us. He is both beloved and friend—both dimensions being necessary for a rich and real relationship.

Reflection

How do you more easily relate to God—as lover and beloved or as friend?

HELEN JULIAN CSF

EXODUS 33:7, 9–11 (NRSV)

Face to face

Now Moses used to take the tent and pitch it outside the camp, far off from the camp; he called it the tent of meeting. And everyone who sought the Lord would go out to the tent of meeting, which was outside the camp... When Moses entered the tent, the pillar of cloud would descend and stand at the entrance of the tent, and the Lord would speak with Moses. When all the people saw the pillar of cloud standing at the entrance of the tent, all the people would rise and bow down, all of them, at the entrance of their tents. Thus the Lord used to speak to Moses face to face, as one speaks to a friend.

This is a story from the early days of the Israelites, when they are wandering through the desert on their way to the promised land. They have no fixed place in which to worship God, no temple, not even yet the ark of the covenant. Instead, they have 'the tent of meeting'. It seems that this was not somewhere in which God was believed to 'dwell' permanently. Rather, it was somewhere he appeared from time to time. The fact that the tent was far from the camp would imply that going there was not something one did lightly.

Moses seems usually to have met God while alone—at the burning bush (Exodus 3:1–6) and on the mountain (24:15–18). Now in the desert, the tent becomes the place of encounter. The implication of this story is that God speaks to Moses in a way which was not available then to anyone else. God speaks in the way that one person speaks to another, rather than through dreams or visions or casting lots.

We believe that, through the coming of Christ, God can now be encountered by anyone and he fills the whole world with his love. Even so, we may still need to take the time to go aside, to leave our 'camp' and make the journey to the place where God can be found and listened to and spoken to.

Reflection

Where is your 'tent of meeting'? How does God speak to you there?

HELEN JULIAN CSF

Costly friendship

But you, Israel my servant, Jacob, whom I have chosen, the off-spring of Abraham, my friend; you whom I took from the ends of the earth, and called from its furthest corners, saying to you, 'You are my servant, I have chosen you and not cast you off'; do not fear, for I am with you, do not be afraid, for I am your God; I will strengthen you, I will help you, I will uphold you with my victorious right hand... You shall seek those who contend with you, but you shall not find them; those who war against you shall be as nothing at all.

This is one of three places in the Bible where Abraham is called God's friend—the others are 2 Chronicles 20:7 and James 2:23. The word translated here as 'friend' can also mean 'beloved'. Whichever word is used, the sense is of a close and warm relationship.

This passage is addressed to people in exile, people in need of reassurance that God has not forgotten them. The prophet brings them an assurance that they are still chosen and God has not forgotten their lineage—they trace their line back to Abraham and God's covenant with him (Genesis 17). For these people, there is nothing ultimately to fear—God is with them, he will protect them and defeat their enemies.

So far so good, but, if we look more closely at Abraham's story, we can see that God's friendship makes demands on him, too—he also has to give and risk. First, he is called to leave his home country and set off for somewhere unknown, when he is already 75 (Genesis 12). Then he is asked to sacrifice his only son, Isaac—the one through whom he has been told he will be the ancestor of many nations. As we know, at the last minute, Isaac is spared (Genesis 22). Abraham might have echoed Teresa of Avila's words to God: 'if this is how you treat your friends, it's no wonder you have so few'!

Reflection
Friendship with God, like grace, is free, but not cheap.
What are you willing to give?

Helen Julian CSF

I call you friends

'This is my commandment, that you love one another as I have loved you. No one has greater love than this, to lay down one's life for one's friends. You are my friends if you do what I command you. I do not call you servants any longer, because the servant does not know what the master is doing; but I have called you friends, because I have made known to you everything that I have heard from my Father. You did not choose me but I chose you. And I appointed you to go and bear fruit, fruit that will last, so that the Father will give you whatever you ask him in my name.'

Here is the central passage for our theme, the one where a whole new way of being is announced. In the Old Testament only a very few exceptional people are called God's friends. Now Jesus, on the eve of his death, speaks to the whole group of his disciples and tells them that they are his friends, despite their frequent misunderstanding of his mission.

This passage follows his words about the 'true vine' (v. 1) and his injunction to 'abide in my love' (v. 9). Love is at the heart of this new relationship of friendship. Jesus' commandment is to love, so the only measure of our entering into this friendship is whether or not we are ready to enter into the love that Jesus shows us, the mutual love of the Trinity which overflows into our lives.

As mentioned in the introduction, in Jesus' time, friendship meant a special open, honest kind of relationship. True friends were those who kept nothing back from each other and, here, Jesus promises that he has held back nothing of what his Father has told him. In Jesus and his teaching, we see God clearly.

Jesus is about to give the ultimate proof of his love by dying for his followers and all who would come to believe through their words, who would be the fruit of their witness. This is not a forced sacrifice, through gritted teeth, but the ultimate expression of friendship.

Prayer

Jesus, as I worship today, help me to believe that you are truly my friend.

HELEN JULIAN CSF

Friendship looks like this

After [Jesus] had washed their feet, had put on his robe, and had returned to the table, he said to them, 'Do you know what I have done to you? You call me Teacher and Lord—and you are right, for that is what I am. So if I, your Lord and Teacher, have washed your feet, you also ought to wash one another's feet. For I have set you an example, that you also should do as I have done to you. Very truly, I tell you, servants are not greater than their master, nor are messengers greater than the one who sent them. If you know these things, you are blessed if you do them.'

This passage comes a little earlier on in John than yesterday's. Jesus has just washed his disciples' feet and now he is teaching them what that surprising act meant. It can be seen as a kind of acted out version of his later teaching on friendship. Also, his laying aside of his robe (13:4) is a foretaste of his laying down his life on the cross.

In undertaking this humble task for them, Jesus shows the disciples a new way in which he is their teacher and Lord—a way of equality. Their relationship is transformed, and he calls on them to follow his example of service, as he will shortly call on them to follow his example of love, love even to death.

This is challenging and radical. It means that Jesus does not stand apart and above everyone else, to be admired, but not imitated. The love that empowered his life is available to empower ours, too, and the mark and test of our friendship with Jesus is not primarily what he does for us, but what we do for him. He never forces the pace, but waits graciously for us to see what he does, be changed by it and so to be enabled to act in new ways.

This is stressed in the final words of this passage: knowing is important, but the blessing comes in doing.

Prayer
Humble God, as you kneel at my feet, help me to not turn away, but learn from your love and put it into practice.

HELEN JULIAN CSF

Partners in service

[The church in Jerusalem] sent Barnabas to Antioch. When he came and saw the grace of God, he rejoiced, and he exhorted them all to remain faithful to the Lord with steadfast devotion; for he was a good man, full of the Holy Spirit and of faith. And a great many people were brought to the Lord. Then Barnabas went to Tarsus to look for Saul, and when he had found him, he brought him to Antioch. So it was that for an entire year they associated with the church and taught a great many people, and it was in Antioch that the disciples were first called 'Christians'.

Here is a well-known example of the importance of human friendship. Barnabas and Saul (later Paul) minister together for a number of chapters in the central section of Acts. At this stage, Barnabas is the senior partner. He vouched for Saul in Jerusalem, when many were still suspicious of this former persecutor who now wanted to join the disciples (9:26–27). Paul recounts a later visit, also with Barnabas, in Galatians 2:1–10.

It is Barnabas who takes the initiative in finding Saul and inviting him to join the church at Antioch. He must have seen the potential in this enthusiastic convert and perhaps their time in Antioch was in some way an apprenticeship for Saul.

Soon, though, the apprentice begins to outdo the teacher. They are sent by the church in Antioch to continue their ministry together and, by the time they reach Lystra, Paul is the 'chief speaker' (Acts 14:12). It is also Paul who is stoned by angry crowds, so he is obviously seen as the main threat. The two return to Antioch together and there, sadly, they fall out and go their separate ways (15:36–41).

Friendship can be a strong basis for ministry, but I wonder how the friendship of Paul and Barnabas was affected by Paul's increasing prominence. Perhaps Barnabas felt sidelined and was, in the end, happy to find a reason to separate from Paul and reclaim a ministry of his own.

Reflection
*Have you experienced or witnessed a friendship taken into ministry
and affected by it? As we remember Barnabas today,
reflect on what you have learnt.*

HELEN JULIAN CSF

End of a friendship

It is not enemies who taunt me—I could bear that; it is not adversaries who deal insolently with me—I could hide from them. But it is you, my equal, my companion, my familiar friend, with whom I kept pleasant company; we walked in the house of God with the throng... But I call upon God, and the Lord will save me. Evening and morning and at noon I utter my complaint and moan, and he will hear my voice.

If the friendship of Barnabas and Saul/Paul changed, here is a friendship that has unequivocally gone wrong. The psalm is one of those classified as a psalm of lament and is a psalm of David, too. However, it does not seem to be linked clearly with any particular incident in David's life, which perhaps makes it easier for us to identify with the feelings of the speaker.

The friendship that has soured is described in powerful phrases. The friend was an equal, sharing the same values and position in the life of the city; a companion, literally one who shared bread with the speaker; a familiar friend, someone known and trusted; pleasant company, so it was an enjoyable relationship, one in which they knew each other's secrets, sealed by sharing together in faith, too. All of this increases the pain of the former friend's present taunts and insolent treatment. Something of the utter bafflement of one whose friend has turned on him comes across in verse 13: 'But it is you...'.

In his distress, the speaker turns to God. He keeps the regular times of prayer ('evening and morning and at noon'), but does not simply repeat formal prayers. Instead, he tells God honestly how he is feeling, complaining and moaning, and is confident that God will hear him.

Sadly, friendships do break down and the better the friendship, the more painful this is. It may be possible to mend it, and it is always worth the attempt, but it may not happen. Human beings are fallible; only God is ultimately faithful.

Prayer

Faithful God, help me to remember that even though others fail me, you will not. Amen

Helen Julian CSF

Shepherd and sheep

'The one who enters by the gate is the shepherd of the sheep. The gatekeeper opens the gate for him, and the sheep hear his voice. He calls his own sheep by name and leads them out.'... So again Jesus said to them, 'Very truly, I tell you, I am the gate for the sheep. All who came before me are thieves and bandits; but the sheep did not listen to them. I am the gate. Whoever enters by me will be saved, and will come in and go out and find pasture. The thief comes only to steal and kill and destroy. I came that they may have life, and have it abundantly. I am the good shepherd. The good shepherd lays down his life for the sheep.'

Here is another passage that sheds light on our friendship with Jesus—and the cost of that friendship. The metaphors get rather mixed—Jesus at different points (10:1–18) is the gate and the shepherd—but the message is clear enough. The good shepherd ('good' here meaning not simply 'good at the job' but also 'ideal') is the one who is willing to die for his sheep. The image of God as a caring shepherd is found in various Old Testament passages—Isaiah 40:11, Jeremiah 23:1–4 and, most powerfully, in Ezekiel 34, especially verses 6 to 11—but in none of them is the shepherd prepared to die for his sheep, although in ancient times that was a real possibility.

In the calling of Jesus' own sheep, we have a vivid picture in his words 'I chose you' (15:16). This is a choice that brings freedom, however, because the sheep are free to 'come in and go out' (10:9), which brings abundant life.

One of the central paradoxes of the Christian faith is that this life comes at the cost of the life of the one whose gift it is. Before he did it, Jesus taught it and left us with memorable images to use as we wrestle with how we live out that dynamic in our own lives as friends of God.

Prayer
Good Shepherd, thank you for your gift of life. Amen

Helen Julian CSF

A friend's betrayal

While [Jesus] was still speaking, Judas, one of the twelve, arrived; with him was a large crowd with swords and clubs, from the chief priests and the elders of the people. Now the betrayer had given them a sign, saying, 'The one I will kiss is the man; arrest him.' At once he came up to Jesus and said, 'Greetings, Rabbi!' and kissed him. Jesus said to him, 'Friend, do what you are here to do.' Then they came and laid hands on Jesus and arrested him.

Jesus and his disciples are together in the garden of Gethsemane—an enclosed garden, which might perhaps remind us of the sheepfold of our last reading. Here, too, there is one who comes to kill and destroy. Judas has become the universal symbol of betrayal in Western culture, even among those who know little of the stories in the Bible.

Judas does not simply betray Jesus to his enemies, he also perverts the gesture of friendship—using a kiss to identify Jesus. Even as he does this, he still calls him 'Rabbi', which means 'teacher', even though he has rejected his teachings.

Some commentators see Jesus' use of the word 'friend' to Judas as him being rather ironic. I am not so sure. Perhaps he is asserting that even if Judas has betrayed their friendship, he, Jesus, will not respond in kind and disown him. Although this is a major rift, perhaps he hopes that Judas can still be brought back into relationship. As we know from a little later in Matthew's Gospel, Judas did indeed repent of what he had done (27:3–5), but instead of turning back to Jesus, he killed himself.

Most of us will probably never experience such a life-or-death betrayal by a friend, although sadly it does still happen in our troubled world, as does the heroism of those who stand by friends, even at great risk to themselves.

The story of Judas can lead us to reflect on how we respond to being let down by friends. Do we hit back or can we still call them 'friends'?

Prayer

God of forgiveness, teach me, like Jesus, to forgive those
who turn against me.

HELEN JULIAN CSF

Friend of sinners

[Jesus said] 'To what then will I compare the people of this generation, and what are they like? They are like children sitting in the
marketplace and calling to one another, "We played the flute for
you, and you did not dance; we wailed, and you did not weep."
For John the Baptist has come eating no bread and drinking no
wine, and you say, "He has a demon"; the Son of Man has come
eating and drinking, and you say, "Look, a glutton and a drunkard,
a friend of tax collectors and sinners!" Nevertheless, wisdom is
vindicated by all her children.'

Some people are never satisfied! Here, Jesus addresses those who found
John too austere to be acceptable as a messenger from God and himself
far too sociable. What is more, he is considered to be socialising with
the wrong people—tax collectors and sinners, those whom John himself may have been referring to as 'the chaff' (3:17), which would be
swept into the fire.

For the religious authorities of Jesus' time, food was an important
way of marking out who and what was holy. The food laws distinguished God's chosen people from the pagans among whom they lived.
Choosing to sit down and eat and drink with those who were deemed
to be 'unclean' put Jesus beyond the pale.

Jesus, though, has a different wisdom, using shared meals as a way
of uniting to himself all who are willing to sit down with him, to share
bread and drink wine (perhaps there is a glimpse ahead to the Eucharist
here) and listen to his words.

For those who were outsiders, this was a radical gift of acceptance. It
was not just the satisfying of their physical need for food but also the
chance to be treated as an individual, someone worth spending time
with, worth listening to. Perhaps this is why shared meals have become
central to much modern evangelism. Jesus offered his friendship to
those who needed it most, in this very concrete way. Those who disap-
proved saw it as a powerful sign, perhaps one that was critical of them.

Reflection
How do you and your church show friendship to outsiders?

HELEN JULIAN CSF

Loving and loved

Now a certain man was ill, Lazarus of Bethany, the village of Mary and her sister Martha. Mary was the one who anointed the Lord with perfume and wiped his feet with her hair; her brother Lazarus was ill. So the sisters sent a message to Jesus, 'Lord, he whom you love is ill.' But when Jesus heard it, he said, 'This illness does not lead to death; rather it is for God's glory, so that the Son of God may be glorified through it.'... After saying this, he told [his disciples], 'Our friend Lazarus has fallen asleep, but I am going there to awaken him.'

Jesus calls his disciples 'friends', but he also seems to have had his own particular circle of friends, those who supported him and perhaps provided some refuge and respite from the demands of his ministry. The household at Bethany—Martha, Mary and Lazarus—appears to have been one such group of friends.

I have chosen this story to represent the various places in which they appear—Jesus' visit to Mary and Martha (Luke 10:38–42), the entire story of Lazarus (John 11:1–44; 12:9–11), the further story of Mary anointing Jesus' feet in John 12:1–8 and the brief mention of Bethany in Matthew 21:17.

Their friendship is no secret: Mary and Martha describe their brother in their message to Jesus as 'he whom you love' (John 11:3). Jesus replies not to them but to his disciples, explaining that Lazarus' illness will not result in his actual death, but in an opportunity for Jesus to manifest the victory over death towards which he is himself moving. His confidence is such that he waits two days before making his way to Bethany.

These three friends of Christ can stand for all of us who have entered into his service and, hence, into his friendship. Perhaps Lazarus stands for believers who have died before Christ's return—which is also all of us and all Christians down the ages. We, too, share in God's victory over death and the belief that whatever happens is not the end, it is only another stage in our journey of faith.

Prayer
God of life, give me confidence in your resurrection power.

HELEN JULIAN CSF

Wisdom's gift

The Lord created me at the beginning of his work, the first of his acts of long ago... When he established the heavens, I was there, when he drew a circle on the face of the deep, when he made firm the skies above, when he established the fountains of the deep, when he assigned to the sea its limit, so that the waters might not transgress his command, when he marked out the foundations of the earth, then I was beside him, like a master worker; and I was daily his delight, rejoicing before him always, rejoicing in his inhabited world and delighting in the human race.

How can we enter into this friendship with God, which Moses and Abraham knew and has been made available to everyone through the coming of Jesus? We find a clue in part of the Apocrypha, where we are told that wisdom 'passes into holy souls and makes them friends of God' (Wisdom of Solomon 7:27).

Wisdom is the speaker in this passage from Proverbs (the whole of chapter 8 is a wonderful speech in her voice). She begins by showing how she helps people to live well, with prudence and intelligence, moves on to rulers, to whom she offers insight and strength, then shows how she has, in fact, always been present, from before the very first moment of creation. She worked side by side with God, not just assisting him in the task of creation but also accompanying him in delight and joy. In some texts 'master worker' is 'little child' and there is a sense of pure childlike joy in this passage.

Later theologians draw on these Wisdom passages in their attempts to describe and explain Christ—'Christology', to use the technical term. Paul sees Jesus as not just the power but also the wisdom of God (1 Corinthians 1:24), so always present with God and sharing in his work of creation and re-creation.

Christ, the wisdom of God, can make us into God's friends. This is always a gift and, as ever, we can ask for this gift, for God loves to give.

Prayer
God of wisdom, in your goodness, send me the gift of friendship with you.
Amen

HELEN JULIAN CSF

2 Kings 9—12

Warning! The chapters from Kings that we shall be looking at are full of killings. People are killed by arrows, tossed out of windows, fed to dogs and have their heads chopped off and put in baskets. Modern sensibilities are tested to the full by this kind of biblical narrative.

To make sense of it, we have to go back about 200 years, to the days of the prophet Samuel. The people were demanding that he give them a king, so they could be like other nations. Samuel consulted the Lord, who told him to warn the people what the consequences would be: exploitation, arbitrary rule, violence (1 Samuel 8:4–22). In the blood-stained narratives of 1 and 2 Kings, we see the terrifying fulfilment of God's warning.

What can we gain from these brutal stories? Perhaps the first lesson is that (as Lord Acton said) 'power tends to corrupt, and absolute power corrupts absolutely'. Most of the kings whose reigns are recorded in Kings failed to use their power with wisdom or restraint. They enjoyed power and it was usually sustained by violence. Our difficulty is that sometimes God not only seems to approve of such behaviour but also actually orders it.

This situation can lead us to draw the wrong conclusion, which is that there are two 'Gods' in the Bible—a 'nasty' one in the Old Testament and a 'nice' one in the New. Of course, there is only one God. The God of Abraham is also the God and Father of Jesus. It is not that God changes, but our human understanding of him grows clearer and brighter as the revelation in scripture progresses. All the while, human minds open to the Spirit and learn more and more about the nature of the God they worship.

The great prophet Elijah was given a very specific remit (1 Kings 19:15–18) and most of the mayhem we shall read about is the consequence of that remit being fulfilled under his successor, Elisha. Jehu was the king chosen to eradicate the insidious cult of Baal. Neither the practices of the cult, nor some of the methods used to counter it, would pass muster at a modern International Court of Human Rights, but that is now and this was then.

David Winter

59

First task fulfilled

Then the prophet Elisha called a member of the company of prophets and said to him, 'Gird up your loins; take this flask of oil in your hand, and go to Ramoth-gilead. When you arrive, look there for Jehu son of Jehoshaphat... Then take the flask of oil, pour it on his head, and say, "Thus says the Lord: I anoint you king over Israel." Then open the door and flee; do not linger.' So the young man, the young prophet, went to Ramoth-gilead... Jehu got up and went inside; the young man poured the oil on his head, saying to him, 'Thus says the Lord the God of Israel: I anoint you king over the people of the Lord, over Israel. You shall strike down the house of your master Ahab, so that I may avenge on Jezebel the blood of my servants the prophets, and the blood of all the servants of the Lord. For the whole house of Ahab shall perish.'

Thus was fulfilled part of the commission that Elijah had been given (1 Kings 19:15–18), though it was being carried out by his successor, Elisha. He was to anoint Jehu, one of the army commanders, as the new king of Israel. It was a risky business and one that Elisha entrusted to a 'young prophet' (2 Kings 9:4) in his company. Notice the instruction he gave him not to linger! The whole 'house of Ahab' was under judgment: it was the family that had not only promoted the worship of Baal but also, urged on by the foreign queen Jezebel, had set out to eliminate all those prophets of the Lord who were brave enough to denounce it.

The worship of Baal was a fertility cult, very widespread among the Canaanite tribes. Why should they not pray for good harvests, though? One problem was that prayers at these shrines were not always addressed to the Lord (Yahweh). They were also for human fertility and could be accompanied by erotic rituals and orgies, sometimes even human sacrifice. Such practices could not be tolerated by the people of the covenant.

Reflection

'You shall fear the Lord your God; him alone you shall worship; to him you shall hold fast, and by his name you shall swear' (Deuteronomy 10:20).

DAVID WINTER

An injustice avenged

Then King Joram of Israel and King Ahaziah of Judah set out, each in his chariot, and went to meet Jehu; they met him at the property of Naboth the Jezreelite. When Joram saw Jehu, he said, 'Is it peace, Jehu?' He answered, 'What peace can there be, so long as the many whoredoms and sorceries of your mother Jezebel continue?' Then Joram reined about and fled, saying to Ahaziah, 'Treason, Ahaziah!' Jehu drew his bow with all his strength, and shot Joram between the shoulders, so that the arrow pierced his heart; and he sank in his chariot. Jehu said to his aide Bidkar, 'Lift him out, and throw him on the plot of ground belonging to Naboth the Jezreelite.'... When King Ahaziah of Judah saw this, he fled... Jehu pursued him, saying 'Shoot him also!'

This is Jehu's first step towards carrying out the command to eliminate the 'house of Ahab'. Joram, then king of Israel, was the son of Ahab and his evil wife Jezebel. Jehu had arranged to meet him, with Ahaziah the king of Judah, who had also dabbled in Baalism. Jehu's intentions soon became obvious and the two kings attempted to ride off, but Joram was killed by a well-aimed arrow and Ahaziah fatally wounded (v. 27).

Jehu instructed his aide to throw the body of Joram on to the plot of land that had once belonged to Naboth. Many years earlier (1 Kings 21—22) Ahab, egged on by Jezebel, had acquired that land by making false accusations of blasphemy against the owner and getting him stoned to death. The king then assumed ownership of the plot, which adjoined his own palace. Elijah confronted him there and warned him that he and his family would be punished for this act of brutality and theft. Dogs would lick his blood in the very place where Naboth's blood had been shed and dogs would eat Jezebel's body. Because Ahab, who was a weak and unprincipled ruler, showed signs of repentance, Elijah postponed these punishments. They would take place after Ahab's death, in the days of Joram. Now that moment had come.

Reflection

Forgive me, Lord, when I excuse my sins as weakness when they are, like Ahab's, my own deliberate fault.

DAVID WINTER

61

2 KINGS 9:30–36 (NRSV, ABRIDGED)

The end of an evil woman

When Jehu came to Jezreel, Jezebel heard of it; she painted her eyes, and adorned her head, and looked out of the window. As Jehu entered the gate, she said, 'Is it peace, Zimri, murderer of your master?' He looked up to the window and said, 'Who is on my side? Who?' Two or three eunuchs looked out at him. He said, 'Throw her down.' So they threw her down; some of her blood spattered on the wall and on the horses, which trampled on her... When they went to bury her, they found no more of her than the skull and the feet and the palms of her hands. When they came back and told him, he said, 'This is the word of the Lord, which he spoke by his servant Elijah the Tishbite, "In the territory of Jezreel the dogs shall eat the flesh of Jezebel."'

Jezebel's end is as colourful and violent as her life had been. She meets her accuser, Jehu, wearing her make-up and adornments, with a cheeky greeting—Zimri was the last man to usurp the throne, but his reign was extremely brief (1 Kings 16:9–20). There then follows a detailed account of her death in which she is tossed from the window by her own servants to die on the pavement below, where dogs ate her flesh. It was, the chronicler would say, an appropriate death for a foreign queen who had corrupted the people of Israel. Not only that, but it was a fulfilment of the prophetic words of the great Elijah.

That is all true, of course, and justice of a crude kind had undoubtedly been done. I think the Christian reader today may recoil from the obvious relish with which every detail is recorded. Joram is dead, Azariah died from wounds received on the day of that fateful meeting with Jehu and now that arch-villain, Jezebel, has met her end. Even so, the cleansing of the land is not yet complete.

Reflection

'Have I any pleasure in the death of the wicked, says the Lord God, and not rather that they should turn from their ways and live?' (Ezekiel 18:23)

DAVID WINTER

A question of means and ends

When [Jehu] left there, he met Jehonadab son of Rechab coming to meet him; he greeted him, and said to him, 'Is your heart as true to mine as mine is to yours?' Jehonadab answered, 'It is.' Jehu said, 'If it is, give me your hand.' So he gave him his hand. Jehu took him up with him into the chariot. He said, 'Come with me, and see my zeal for the Lord.' So he had him ride in his chariot. When he came to Samaria, he killed all who were left to Ahab in Samaria, until he had wiped them out, according to the word of the Lord that he spoke to Elijah.

'There' in the first verse refers to Jezreel, a valley between Galilee and Samaria and a centre for the worship of Baal during the years of Ahab's reign. The first 14 verses of this chapter are not for sensitive dispositions. According to Stephen Dawes in his 'People's Bible Commentary' on 1 and 2 Kings (BRF, 2001, p. 150), they describe 'one of the most gruesome sights in the whole of Kings' (and that is saying something). It involved the killing of the younger generation of the household of Ahab. Jezreel was now 'cleansed'.

That left Samaria to be dealt with. For this, Jehu—who sees his actions as evidence of his 'zeal for the Lord'—acquired another assistant, a man called Jehonadab. Together they rode into Samaria in Jehu's famous chariot ('he drives like a maniac', we are told at 9:20) and proceeded to kill 'all who were left to Ahab in Samaria' (10:17). The killing is not yet complete, as we shall see, but the chronicler adds the words of justification here: 'according to the word of the Lord that he spoke to Elijah' (v. 17).

It may be that these mass killings were the only way to deal with the menace of Baalism. We shall see later, though, that the next king of Judah found a way to reclaim the people for the Lord which did not involve multiple slaughter.

Reflection

The 'word of the Lord... to Elijah' (v. 17) dealt with outcomes; the tactics of Jehu were concerned with means. That is an important distinction.

DAVID WINTER

A cunning plan

Jehu sent word throughout all Israel; all the worshippers of Baal came, so that there was no one left who did not come... Then Jehu entered the temple of Baal with Jehonadab son of Rechab; he said to the worshippers of Baal, 'Search and see that there is no worshipper of the Lord here among you, but only worshippers of Baal.' Then they proceeded to offer sacrifices and burnt-offerings. Now Jehu had stationed eighty men outside, saying, 'Whoever allows any of those to escape whom I deliver into your hands shall forfeit his life.' As soon as he had finished presenting the burnt-offering, Jehu said to the guards and to the officers, 'Come in and kill them; let no one escape.' So they put them to the sword... Then they demolished the pillar of Baal, and destroyed the temple of Baal, and made it a latrine to this day. Thus Jehu wiped out Baal from Israel.

Now we see Jehu the cunning plotter at work. He announced that he was 'for' Baal—more so even than Ahab—and invited all Baal's followers to join him for celebrations in the cult's temple. Once the crowds arrived (how gullible can you be?), the doors were shut. At the appointed time the massacre began, carried out by Jehu's guards posted at the doors. The temple was destroyed, its idolatrous objects of devotion desecrated and its site made into a public toilet.

So Jehu completed the task for which he was chosen. Baalism had been eradicated (for a time) from the whole of Israel. Although clearly he had 'done well in carrying out what I [the Lord] consider right' (v. 30), and for this it was promised that his sons would sit on the throne of Israel for four generations, the overall verdict of the chronicler is not perfect. Jehu removed Baal, but he left the idolatrous golden calves in Bethel and Dan (v. 29). Jehu reigned in Israel for 28 years, eventually, unlike most of his victims, dying peacefully—he 'slept with his ancestors' (v. 35).

Reflection

Good, but far from perfect—though that might be God's verdict on most of us!

DAVID WINTER

Hidden in the house of the Lord

Sunday 23 June

2 KINGS 11:1–4 (NRSV)

Now when Athaliah, Ahaziah's mother, saw that her son was dead, she set about to destroy all the royal family. But Jehosheba, King Joram's daughter, Ahaziah's sister, took Joash son of Ahaziah, and stole him away from among the king's children who were about to be killed; she put him and his nurse in a bedroom. Thus she hid him from Athaliah, so that he was not killed; he remained with her for six years, hidden in the house of the Lord, while Athaliah reigned over the land. But in the seventh year Jehoiada summoned the captains of the Carites and of the guards and had them come to him in the house of the Lord. He made a covenant with them and put them under oath in the house of the Lord; then he showed them the king's son.

We now go back a while, to pick up events in the southern kingdom of Judah. King Ahaziah had died from a wound inflicted by Jehu's arrow, but, instead of one of his sons taking his place, his mother, Athaliah, took control. This involved (yet again) slaughter on a large scale as she ordered the killing of all the king's sons—he would have had many wives, of course. Once again, we see the corrupting attraction of power. However, unknown to her, one son, a toddler at the time, evaded the executions, hidden in a room in the temple courts by his aunt and a faithful nurse. This little boy, Joash, also enjoyed the protection of the priest Jehoiada and, when he reached the age of seven, plans were laid for a coup and a coronation.

This story has overtones of the hiding of Moses from the Egyptians. Could God's people be liberated and blessed once again by a young boy raised in royal circles, but secretly? The time was certainly overdue for the emergence of a good king, one who was wisely advised by a faithful priest of the Lord.

Reflection

There is something very moving about the thought of being 'hidden in the house of the Lord'. It might remind us of the closing words of Psalm 23:
'I shall dwell in the house of the Lord my whole life long.'

DAVID WINTER

The Fourth Sunday after Trinity 65

2 Kings 11:12, 17–20 (NRSV, abridged)

The coronation of the boy king

Then [Jehoiada] brought out the king's son, put the crown on him, and gave him the covenant; they proclaimed him king, and anointed him; they clapped their hands and shouted, 'Long live the king!'... Jehoiada made a covenant between the Lord and the king and people, that they should be the Lord's people; also between the king and the people. Then all the people of the land went to the house of Baal, and tore it down; his altars and his images they broke in pieces, and they killed Mattan, the priest of Baal, before the altars... Then they brought the king down from the house of the Lord, marching through the gate of the guards to the king's house. He took his seat on the throne of the kings. So all the people of the land rejoiced; and the city was quiet after Athaliah had been killed with the sword at the king's house.

In Judah, the scene has dramatically changed. The boy king, Joash, now aged just seven, is solemnly crowned and installed as king, with the priest Jehoida presiding over the arrangements. In contrast to all the power-hungry monarchs who had served this land and Israel so badly for many years, the account of these events continually refers to 'the people' (six times in verses 17–20). This is an element that has been singularly lacking, yet the kingdoms of Israel were meant to be built on the basis of a willing partnership between the ruler and his subjects. Jehoiada, in his wisdom, was seeking to redress the balance of power in the land. It was to be a covenant between the Lord, the king and the people, not a device to enable one man (or, as had happened, one woman) to exercise absolute and arbitrary power.

It is also striking that, in the new scenario, it was the people, not the king, his soldiers or his servants, who destroyed the temple of Baal—and only one person, the Baalite priest, was killed.

Reflection

How many lives might have been spared if Jehu had employed the wisdom of a man like Jehoiada? 'All the people of the land' had rejected Baal. Hallelujah!

David Winter

Listening to the Law of God

In the seventh year of Jehu, Jehoash began to reign; he reigned for forty years in Jerusalem. His mother's name was Zibiah of Beer-sheba. Jehoash did what was right in the sight of the Lord all his days, because the priest Jehoiada instructed him. Nevertheless, the high places were not taken away; the people continued to sacrifice and make offerings on the high places.

Well, if you start young you have got a good chance of a long innings, even in the volatile world of the ninth century BC! So the seven-year-old Joash (now named Jehoash) ruled Judah for 40 years. He is one of the handful of kings in these books who earns the commendation that he 'did what was right in the sight of the Lord all his days' (v. 2)—an enviable testimony indeed. If that is (as it surely should be) every Christian's aim, we might note the role of the wise priest Jehoiada. The young king 'did what was right' because he was 'instructed' by him. I do not think the need for that kind of wise support only applies to young people—however old we are, it can be a great blessing to have someone, or several people, from whom we know we will receive wise counsel.

No one is perfect, however. Even the good king Jehoash failed in one regard: he did not take away the 'high places', where people continued to offer worship and sacrifices. These 'high places' are mentioned right back in the days of the patriarchs—indeed, Jacob set one up at Bethel to be 'God's house' after his dream of a heavenly ladder (Genesis 28:18–22), as did Joshua at Gilgal after the crossing of the Jordan (Joshua 4:20–24). However, after the building of Solomon's temple these 'high places' were seen as providing opportunities for Canaanite and Baalite worship and, as such, were regularly denounced by the prophets. Jehoash was not the only king who failed to remove them—they continue to be seen as threats to the purity of Israel's worship for many centuries.

Prayer

Lord God, help me to be humble enough to listen to good counsel and wise enough to follow it. Amen

David Winter

Caring for the Lord's house

Then the priest Jehoiada took a chest, made a hole in its lid, and set it beside the altar on the right side as one entered the house of the Lord; the priests who guarded the threshold put in it all the money that was brought into the house of the Lord… They would give the money that was weighed out into the hands of the workers who had the oversight of the house of the Lord; then they paid it out to the carpenters and the builders who worked on the house of the Lord, to the masons and the stonecutters, as well as to buy timber and quarried stone for making repairs on the house of the Lord, as well as for any outlay for repairs of the house.

You may notice that 'Lord' is often printed in the Bible in capital letters. That is highly significant because it shows the writer is speaking of Yahweh, the revealed identity of the one true God (Exodus 3:13–14, God reveals this name to Moses). There were many 'lords' and many 'gods' in the ancient world—indeed, 'Baal' means 'lord'. It was not a matter of whether or not you served a 'lord', but which Lord you served!

All this meant that maintaining the temple, the house of the Lord God (Yahweh), was crucial. It was only there that the people could be sure of finding genuine worship of the one true God. Jehoiada made sure that the practical business of repairing the temple was carried out, in terms of both fundraising and physical work. The people made their gifts, the priests guarded them carefully and then passed them on to the skilled workers who cared for the building.

For us, the 'house of the Lord' is not simply a building (though it may be, of course), but maintaining, in a public way, true worship and witness to the one eternal God, the Father of our Lord Jesus. Frankly, every church needs a Jehoiada!

Reflection

The church where we gather is simply an empty shrine unless it is filled with the beauty of sincere and holy worship.

DAVID WINTER

Dealing honestly

But for the house of the Lord no basins of silver, snuffers, bowls, trumpets, or any vessels of gold, or of silver, were made from the money that was brought into the house of the Lord, for that was given to the workers who were repairing the house of the Lord with it. [The king's secretary and the high priest] did not ask for an account from those into whose hand they delivered the money to pay out to the workers, for they dealt honestly. The money from the guilt-offerings and the money from the sin-offerings was not brought into the house of the Lord; it belonged to the priests.

It is a sad fact that, every year, there are stories in local and national newspapers of treasurers and officials who have been found out as having failed the test of scrupulous honesty where church finances are concerned. We read in the New Testament that 'The love of money is a root of all kinds of evil' (1 Timothy 6:10). Along with power and lust, money can indeed be a deadly destroyer of Christian integrity.

So it is encouraging to see that the temple regime initiated by the redoubtable Jehoiada encompassed such high standards of personal honesty that no 'accounting' was asked for or even expected, because 'they dealt honestly' (v. 15). Those who engaged the workers, as well as the workers themselves who were entrusted with the sacred task of repairing the temple of the Lord, were trustworthy. Clearly Jehoida and the other officials knew what they were doing—even the risk they might be running—but their confidence proved to be justified.

Personal honesty of this kind is much praised in Psalms and Proverbs as the true evidence of righteousness, a sign that we are doing what God requires. It is no less so for Christians in the 21st century. Doing tax returns, expenses claims, repaying debts, handing in money or valuables found in the street—these are modern tests of the kind of honesty that the Lord expects of us.

Reflection

'Honest balances and scales are the Lord's; all the weights in the bag are his work' (Proverbs 16:11).

David Winter

An error of judgment

At that time King Hazael of Aram went up, fought against Gath, and took it. But when Hazael set his face to go up against Jerusalem, King Jehoash of Judah took all the votive gifts that Jehoshaphat, Jehoram, and Ahaziah, his ancestors, the kings of Judah, had dedicated, as well as his own votive gifts, all the gold that was found in the treasuries of the house of the Lord and of the king's house, and sent these to King Hazael of Aram. Then Hazael withdrew from Jerusalem.

We have already learnt that Hazael, the king of Aram (the lands that lay to the north of Israel), had begun to 'trim off' regions of Israel 'from the Jordan eastwards', in punishment, it seems, for King Jehu's failure to 'follow the law of the Lord… with all his heart' (10:31–32). Now he began to turn his attention to the southern kingdom, Judah. By this time, the 'boy king' Joash would have been in his forties and, we may assume, his long-time mentor Jehoiada had died. Faced with this powerful invading force, which had already conquered Gath and captured some of the territory of Israel and without the wise priest to turn to for counsel, the king panicked. Raiding the temple treasury and also his own storerooms of riches, he gathered together a priceless tribute, which he then paid to the aggressor Hazael. In response, Hazael withdrew his troops so that Joash was able to retain his throne. However, the price paid was humiliating and also sacrilegious, for some of the treasures he had taken to pay off Hazael were 'votive' gifts, dedicated to the Lord.

Many years earlier, Elijah had been instructed by the Lord to anoint Hazael as king of Aram (1 Kings 19:15). He was to be, with Jehu, an agent of God's judgment on the sins of Israel and Judah. In strange ways, the story unfolds.

Reflection

Not surprisingly for one who took the throne as a young boy,
Joash had relied heavily on his counsellor, Jehoiada. Taking advice is good,
but sooner or later each of us has to learn to make our own decisions
and live by their consequences.

DAVID WINTER

Fatally flawed

Now the rest of the acts of Joash, and all that he did, are they not written in the Book of the Annals of the Kings of Judah? His servants arose, devised a conspiracy, and killed Joash in the house of Millo, on the way that goes down to Silla. It was Jozacar son of Shimeath and Jehozabad son of Shomer, his servants, who struck him down, so that he died. He was buried with his ancestors in the city of David; then his son Amaziah succeeded him.

We have already been told that Joash 'did what was right in the sight of the Lord all his days', but also that he failed to remove the 'high places', the sacrificial sites outside Jerusalem. While Jehoiada was beside him as mentor and counsellor (and while he accepted that guidance), it seems that all went well. Sadly, though, as we have seen, when faced with a major national emergency, he chose to compromise on his principles rather than face the enemy head on. Perhaps that was his fatal flaw—an element of indecision—plus the typical kingly ambition to cling to power at all costs.

The penalty was to become the victim of a coup by his own familiar servants. It is sad to see a reign that was, for most of its 40 years, faithful and good end in disappointment and assassination. I suppose it is not fanciful to see this as being the case for any life that does not entirely fulfil its God-given potential.

Many of us who are in our 'senior' years may have regrets about unfulfilled ambitions and times when we, like Joash, have been deaf to the voice of God. It is comforting that he was still buried with honour in the city of his ancestor David and his acts are 'written in the Book of the Annals of the Kings of Judah'.

Reflection

A secret of a happy life is to turn regrets into gratitude. Joash might have died as a baby, but for a brave aunt and a faithful nurse. He might have failed in his early reign, but for the wise Jehoiada. Each of us, like him, can look back and give thanks.

DAVID WINTER

1 and 2 Timothy

The letters of Paul to Timothy are often considered the 'poor relatives'. Complaints such as 'they're not as exciting as Romans' or 'not as sharp as Galatians' often see them relegated to the third division. Worse still, they have been described as alien to Paul's own teaching. Why is this and are these criticisms fair? In the next few days, we will explore these letters and examine their themes, complaints and hopes and expose this view to scrutiny. We can assess for ourselves if they speak to us afresh and the 'glorious gospel' (1 Timothy 1:11) still has the power to captivate and inspire us.

What, then, of the suggestion that these letters, often called (with the letter to Titus) 'the Pastorals', are not from Paul? Some comment that the language used here is different from Paul's other letters. Do the letters *sound* as though Paul wrote them? Also, they appear to describe a situation that some think is different from the one Paul was actually facing—the life of the church seems more regulated than we see in his other letters, so these letters relate to a period that is different from Paul's lifetime. Where are the lofty statements of faith, such as we see in Romans 8 or Galatians 5? Are these letters lacking that essentially 'Pauline punch' which helps us identify them as his?

These are good questions, but they raise other problems, too, and are not, in fact, without answers. First, both letters claim to come from Paul and show clear signs of personal information, such as concerning Timothy's family (2 Timothy 1:5). It is also very likely that these letters are later than others and language use does change. Have you ever read a letter you wrote many years earlier and noticed how different you sound? Finally, the aims and themes of 1 and 2 Timothy may be different from the other letters because these are addressed to a person, not to a church. This alone could explain their distinctiveness.

Whatever our conclusions, we ought to read these letters anew. The author claims that all scripture is inspired by God (2 Timothy 3:16). With prayerful openness, let us together listen to what the Spirit is saying to the Church.

Andrew John

1 TIMOTHY 1:1–4 (NIV, ABRIDGED)

Greetings and goals

Paul, an apostle of Christ Jesus by the command of God our Saviour and of Christ Jesus our hope, to Timothy my true son in the faith: Grace, mercy and peace from God the Father and Christ Jesus our Lord... Command certain people not to teach false doctrines any longer or to devote themselves to myths and endless genealogies. Such things promote controversial speculations rather than advancing God's work—which is by faith.

If there is one thing you can guarantee in Paul's letters it is the lack of small talk! Our letter kicks off with Paul identifying himself and addressing Timothy as his true child in the faith. This is a personal letter between two servants of God whose strong commitment to one another is founded on their common faith, but it is not a round robin, with the year's news, slightly exaggerated, retold for effect. This letter has a definite aim of encouraging Timothy in his ministry and providing clear guidance for some difficult decisions.

I love the phrase a 'red herring'. Apparently, it dates back to the time when a pungent kipper would be used to provide an alternative but false scent to train hounds not to swerve from their task of seeking out a fox. As Paul begins his letter, he exposes some red herrings that appear to have swayed a number of Christians from the true path. His aim is to get to the heart of what underpins our faith, so, in verse 5, we read, 'The goal of this command is love, which comes from a pure heart and a good conscience and a sincere faith.'

This is a message that brooks no obstacles. What makes it compelling is the authority of the writer, who is 'an apostle of Christ Jesus by the command of God our Saviour' (v. 1). As we start to read this letter, we might pause and ask if we will allow the serious issues of faith to lead and guide us rather than being diverted by what may seem interesting but actually turns out to be unhelpful.

Prayer

Lord, give me a heart and mind that holds firm the important matters of faith and is not distracted by lesser matters, for the sake of Jesus. Amen

ANDREW JOHN

The need for patience

Here is a trustworthy saying that deserves full acceptance: Christ Jesus came into the world to save sinners—of whom I am the worst. But for that very reason I was shown mercy so that in me, the worst of sinners, Christ Jesus might display his immense patience as an example for those who would believe in him and receive eternal life. Now to the King eternal, immortal, invisible, the only God, be honour and glory for ever and ever. Amen

'Patience is a virtue' goes the saying, although acquiring it is a good deal harder than stating it! In this part of his letter, Paul urges Timothy to hold the faith and 'fight the battle well' (vv. 18–20), in accordance with prophecies made about him. This kind of exhortation needs unpacking and Paul does this by emphasising the seriousness of an uncontrolled life and offers real hope from his own experience.

He begins with an explanation of why the Law is needed (vv. 9–10): it exposes human sin for what it really is and allows no excuses nor escape route. This kind of analysis is uncompromising and at odds with a society that can describe behaviour uncritically, as though it were all morally neutral. Without the recognition that sin is destructive, though, Paul could not sing God's praises (v. 17) because it was to such a sinner that Christ revealed himself and, despite the sin, displayed in him his 'immense patience as an example' (v. 16). So, we see two great biblical themes present here—law and grace, which both work in the mercy of God. What makes this message powerful is that Paul does not commend himself as virtuous but simply as one in whom God's goodness has taken root. The patience of Christ has found the patient Paul who knows that he is in need of healing. We need this kind of reflection and perspective so that we never forget the emptiness of our lives apart from God nor the amazing grace that saved us.

Prayer

Lord, you have shown me the path to life and healed me. Give me grace today to live that life in the light of your grace and forgiveness, for Christ's sake. Amen

ANDREW JOHN

1 TIMOTHY 2:1–2, 5–7 (TNIV, ABRIDGED)

Making connections

I urge, then, first of all, that petitions, prayers, intercession and thanksgiving be made for everyone—for kings and all those in authority, that we may live peaceful and quiet lives in all godliness and holiness... For there is one God and one mediator between God and human beings, Christ Jesus, himself human, who gave himself as a ransom for all people... And for this purpose I was appointed a herald and an apostle... and a true and faithful teacher of the Gentiles.

My wife is a devotee of Hercule Poirot and I have always been fascinated by the way in which he connects the evidence with the solution, so that the murderer is revealed. Connections are important in today's passage, too, and necessary if our discipleship is to make sense. Paul has been outlining the basis of faith—that Jesus saves us from sin and makes us God's own people. Here he begins to draw out the implications of this, beginning with prayer (v. 1)—specifically, intercessory prayer for 'everyone', but especially those in high positions. The confidence for this comes from Christ himself, who mediates between God and people (v. 5).

Paul has three good reasons for starting with prayer. First, because prayer is the beginning and, without it, we might miss what God is doing or even experience what many call the 'tarrying' of God, which is when no answers seem forthcoming, until we pray, that is. Second, because prayer can change society and those within it. We must never imagine our world is 'beyond the pale' or resort to a kind of 'tut-tut' Christianity where there is much shaking of the head over the state of things, but not enough bowing of the knee. Third, because, as Paul discovered, Jesus is wonderfully patient and able to exercise the same saving grace in others that he worked in him. There is no place here for despair. Making the connection between Christ's grace and the needs of the world is the basis for faithful, persistent prayer.

Prayer

Lord, I turn to you and know you hear me. May I discover what you will and seek it with a renewed heart, soul and mind for the honour of your name. Amen

ANDREW JOHN

Working it out

I do not permit a woman to teach or to assume authority… Adam was not the one deceived; it was the woman who was deceived and became a sinner. But women will be saved through childbearing—if they continue in faith, love and holiness with propriety.

Having begun with prayer, Paul moves on to its practices and how worship should be conducted. This allows us to see that faith informs discipleship, but why does Paul give more attention to advising women? The answer lies in other parts of the letter (5:3–16), in which difficult pastoral matters are addressed. It appears that women were behaving in a way that reflected badly on the church and Christ as a consequence. For example, fine hair and pearls (2:9) may not be significant in themselves, but, if what they signified offended in relation to the message of the gospel, they were to be discouraged—likewise, women teaching or exercising authority.

Paul bolsters his point with reference to scripture (vv. 13–14), which is important because he was not interested in winning an argument but in living according to the truth. More positively, he states that women should pour their energies into creative acts. If these reflect a life of devotion to Christ, they can be assured of salvation (v. 15).

What are we to make of this today? It would be easy to dismiss it as the thinking of another culture and assign it no place at all in 21st-century Christianity. It would also be too easy to read this 'straight', without any thought given to culture and change. What controls Paul's thinking is Christ and the new order of the kingdom. Whatever gives shape to the values of the kingdom must prevail in the lives of Christian people and not the culture of the age or the desires of individuals. Our situation—and our understanding of the role of women and men—is very different from Paul's but the kingdom remains. This is the reality and the truth we must apprehend.

Prayer

Lord Jesus, may your church be ordered and nurtured in such a way that your kingdom may be seen more clearly, for your greater glory. Amen

Andrew John

Right leading

Here is a trustworthy saying: whoever aspires to be an overseer desires a noble task. Now the overseer is to be above reproach, faithful to his wife, temperate, self-controlled, respectable, hospitable, able to teach, not given to drunkenness, not violent but gentle, not quarrelsome, not a lover of money. He must manage his own family well and see that his children obey him, and he must do so in a manner worthy of full respect. (If anyone does not know how to manage his own family, how can he take care of God's church?)

When our children were very young, we had a room that we called 'the spare room'. In truth, it filled up with all the things we were not sure about keeping, but did not want to throw out. I remember being unable to access the room once because too much clutter had fallen on the inside behind the door! It was chaotic and became unmanageable. In today's passage, Paul continues to give clear instruction to avoid this kind of disorder and the lifestyles that discredit the gospel.

The passage begins by saying that it is a noble aspiration to lead (v. 1), then continues with positive messages about how leaders are to manage their personal environment (v. 4). We must not lose sight of these messages in the more tightly phrased constraints concerning money or alcohol (v. 3). Once more we should understand that the values of the kingdom are central here—there is to be no gap between the public and private spheres. The willingness of a leader to be disciplined affects not only the quality of that ministry but also how it is perceived by others.

This is a powerful message and not just for the church, because it gets to the heart of what can be identified as being properly authentic. When leaders' personal lives are at odds with their public ministry, the gospel and the church, as well as those leaders, are compromised. It is strong but wise instruction; a 'noble task' requires noble service and faithfulness.

Prayer

Lord, give us wise leaders whose lives and ministry are all of a piece:
may your church be blessed through them. Amen

ANDREW JOHN

Serving in life and the church

In the same way, deacons are to be worthy of respect, sincere, not indulging in much wine, and not pursuing dishonest gain. They must keep hold of the deep truths of the faith with a clear conscience. They must first be tested; and then if there is nothing against them, let them serve as deacons. In the same way, the women are to be worthy of respect, not malicious talkers but temperate and trustworthy in everything.

If Paul wishes to encourage a strong faith environment in his leaders, he is equally committed to the task of nurturing and exhorting deacons, whose roles, if not completely clear, appear to be to support their leaders. He commends the same kind of discipline in all areas of life, therefore, including appetites (v. 8) and personal relationships (vv. 11–12).

Having said this, he adds two important elements worth exploring. First, there is the way in which they hold their convictions and their conduct together (v. 9). The 'deep truths of the faith' are undoubtedly the gospel and how the overflowing grace of God (1:14) does not give us licence to continue in self-serving lifestyles, but, rather, causes us to live as Christ lived. Paul is again making connections between the confession of faith and the life of the Christian disciple. Second, he encourages Timothy to test those who are called to this service (3:10). This is important because discernment is a key part of life for every Christian, whether in relation to big issues in life or much smaller matters. The aim is to discover the will of Christ and sometimes this is revealed in the way people perform the tasks given to them.

Jesus taught that how gifts are used reveals a great deal about a person's character (Matthew 25:14–30) and Paul's wise and judicious counsel sounds similar. As with overseers, deacons represent not just themselves but also Christ their Saviour—we cannot embrace the ministry of Christ without embracing the life of Christ.

Prayer

Lord, I pray for all who are discerning your call to serve. Guide, protect them and uphold them so they may honour and uplift you, for Jesus' sake. Amen

ANDREW JOHN

God's future—joy and challenge

> Beyond all question, the mystery from which true godliness springs is great: He appeared in the flesh, was vindicated by the Spirit, was seen by angels, was preached among the nations, was believed on in the world, was taken up in glory... For everything God created is good, and nothing is to be rejected if it is received with thanksgiving, because it is consecrated by the word of God and prayer.

In today's passage, we see Paul tying the call to godliness to some of the great truths about Jesus. Previously, his emphasis has been on personal and public conduct, but here he shifts to moral considerations, such as marriage, eating certain foods and how we should understand those who reject such things. The key to this is the puzzling but beautiful hymn (or poem) in 3:16, which shows that everything in life hinges on the person of Jesus. We must relate all we do directly to him.

What are the key elements? First, there is a clear pointer to the identity of Jesus—the 'mystery', which must be a reference to the eternal existence of Christ, whom Christians believe was 'begotten not made' (Nicene Creed). Then follow five descriptions of periods in the Lord's life and this is where the difficulties begin! Does vindication by the Spirit and being seen by angels refer to the resurrection and glorification or events in the life of Jesus, such as his baptism and temptation or anguish in the garden of Gethsemane? It is impossible to be sure and, in fact, both are possible! If, though, 'taken up in glory' refers to his ascension, I incline to the latter view, so his being 'preached among the nations' refers also to those who came to believe in him prior to the ascension.

Whichever view is true, we are reminded that God's vindicated Son is an example of godly living because of who he is and what his life, death and resurrection mean for the church and the world.

Prayer
All praise to you, true and living God, because you have raised and glorified your Son Jesus, who is the hope of all nations.
May his reign grow in me today. Amen

ANDREW JOHN

1 TIMOTHY 4:8–12, 16 (NIV, ABRIDGED)

The better way

> Physical training is of some value, but godliness has value for all things, holding promise for both the present life and the life to come... That is why we labour and strive, because we have put our hope in the living God, who is the Saviour of all people, and especially of those who believe. Command and teach these things. Don't let anyone look down on you because you are young, but set an example for the believers... Watch your life and doctrine closely. Persevere in them, because if you do, you will save both yourself and your hearers.

I remember spending freezing cold afternoons playing on the wing as a rugby player at school. More often than not, someone would drop the ball before it ever reached me! I also remember the oft-repeated phrase, usually shouted at the forwards as they tried to retain possession of the ball, 'use it or lose it'.

In today's passage, Paul returns to his key message about following Christ, but introduces a new way of emphasising this: he compares the discipline of faith with that of the athlete. His instruction to Timothy is that gifts must be cultivated if he is to succeed (see vv. 13–16). He, too, must 'use it or lose it'.

This emphasis has two further aspects. The first is diligence. Timothy must devote himself to teaching and persist in it. We can surely relate to this and know how easy it can be to give up. Paul encourages a steady and determined resolve to work at it for his sake and that of others (v. 16). Second, his life must be an example—he must model the life of Christ so that his faith is commended, despite his youth (v. 12). These are important messages for the church today, too—we must be known as people of integrity whose teaching and lifestyle are harmonious. There is no short cut; it requires commitment and patience and the will to use it or lose it.

Prayer

Help me to use the gifts you have given, Lord, for the sake of others and for the blessing of your world, for Jesus' sake. Amen

ANDREW JOHN

1 Timothy 5:1–2, 11–13 (NIV, abridged)

Laws that love

Do not rebuke an older man harshly, but exhort him as if he were your father. Treat younger men as brothers, older women as mothers, and younger women as sisters, with absolute purity... As for younger widows, do not put them on... a list [of widows]. For when their sensual desires overcome their dedication to Christ, they want to marry. Thus they bring judgment on themselves, because they have broken their first pledge. Besides, they get into the habit of being idle and going about from house to house. And... they become idlers... saying things they ought not to.

Instructions for household appliances are, I suspect, very often ignored, which may have serious consequences! Such things are provided to assist us and the instructions are to help us avoid potential hazards, although our instinct may still be to 'work it out on our own'.

In today's passage, Paul provides instructions to avoid some of life's hazards and ensure that the church is properly ordered as a community. The rules are constructed to ensure justice and fairness for the believing congregation, relating to family members in different ways.

We can see two critical principles at work here. Notice how strongly Paul employs the idea of loving respect in relation to older people (vv. 1–3). Today, the concept of caring for the vulnerable must still guide the church's approach to mission and service. The other principle here is that of personal responsibility. For those in need, there must be loving, practical support, whereas for those who have the capacity and energy for work, there is the command to give themselves in service and avoid being idle (vv. 11, 13).

Our own situation is very different from Paul's and we should be careful not to read this passage as a simple and straightforward template for our churches. Instead, we need to reimagine and reapply the enduring ideas to our context. What kind of church would we have if loving care and mutual responsibility were more visibly present?

Prayer

Teach us to use all our energies and imagination for the good of people and respond positively to your call, true and gracious God. Amen

Andrew John

Disciplines and desires

Do not entertain an accusation against an elder unless it is brought by two or three witnesses. But those elders who are sinning you are to reprove before everyone, so that the others may take warning. I charge you, in the sight of God and Christ Jesus and the elect angels, to keep these instructions without partiality, and to do nothing out of favouritism... All who are under the yoke of slavery should consider their masters worthy of full respect, so that God's name and our teaching may not be slandered.

Here, Paul extends his treatment of discipleship and the call to radical holy living. Once again, we need to be conscious of cultural changes that have occurred since in relation to, for instance, his treatment of slavery. No one would seriously argue that slavery and Christianity are compatible, but it is not the issue that Paul is addressing here. He focuses, rather, on the matter of public sin and some of the real dangers associated with both accusations and ignoring them.

Paul appears very conscious that accusations can be damaging for those from whom much is expected (vv. 17–19). His approach is to offer a test so that false accusations cannot easily smear or destroy someone's reputation. This again harks back to Paul's approach to justice, which should offer protection to the innocent as well as punishment for the guilty. If an overly zealous and hasty approach to sin is one danger, the other is ignoring it. Paul advocates direct confrontation: let sin be uncovered and exposed for what it is.

What, then, of slavery? Paul does not argue against the practice because his concern is not so much with institutional reform as strengthening the witness of believers. The act of honouring one's masters brings credit, above all, to Christ and therefore commends him to the world. There can, however, be little doubt that the overriding message of scripture is for us to have a deeper respect for human freedom and equality before God—a world in which slavery can have no place.

Prayer
Heavenly Father, guide your church so that we are places of justice and fairness where grace and integrity sit together in all we do. Amen

ANDREW JOHN

Rich in life and love

Godliness with contentment is great gain. For we brought nothing into the world, and we can take nothing out of it. But if we have food and clothing, we will be content with that. Those who want to get rich fall into temptation and a trap and into many foolish and harmful desires that plunge people into ruin and destruction. For the love of money is a root of all kinds of evil. Some people, eager for money, have wandered from the faith and pierced themselves with many griefs.

The Bible has a great deal to say about possessions as both gift and danger to God's people. The theme of contentment goes back to the Old Testament (think of Israel's complaints in the wilderness) and it is not surprising to find it here. Today's passage considers the matter of appreciating gifts and how we should deal with one matter especially —money!

For Paul, any rejection of the gospel is not only a matter of error but also results in a gnawing discontentment that only deepens the sense of ruin (v. 9). Notice he does not say money is a root of all evil, nor that it is the root of all evil, but, rather, the love of money is 'a root of all kinds of evils'. The alternative to being consumed by unhealthy appetites is a contentment that comes from godliness (v. 6). How do we cultivate such an attitude? Paul advances the idea that we appreciate our mortality (v. 7) and also the relative worth of material things (v. 8). This careful injunction is radically countercultural because it opposes the 'have more' mentality that has infected much of our world.

Does this mean that the ambition to succeed and receive appropriate reward is wrong? By no means—Paul has earlier stated that the labourer deserves his wages (5:18). Ambition can be worthy and lead to huge advances for many, but it needs to be qualified and guided by the contentment that comes from the gospel giving us a wider outlook and eternal perspective.

Prayer

Lord, you have given us so much. Today, help us to appreciate this and become generous with all you have given, for Christ's sake. Amen

ANDREW JOHN

Leading and learning

But you, man of God... pursue righteousness, godliness, faith, love, endurance and gentleness. Fight the good fight of the faith. Take hold of the eternal life to which you were called... In the sight of God, who gives life to everything, and of Christ Jesus, who while testifying before Pontius Pilate made the good confession, I charge you to keep this command without spot or blame until the appearing of our Lord Jesus Christ, which God will bring about in his own time—God, the blessed and only Ruler, the King of kings and Lord of lords, who alone is immortal and who lives in unapproachable light, whom no one has seen or can see.

Today's passage focuses on the issue of having an eternal perspective, which was the idea that we concluded our meditations with yesterday. Not only does it include a beautiful acclamation of praise (vv. 15–16) but also the verse on which one of the great English hymns is based—'Fight the good fight' (v. 12). Timothy is encouraged to fight this good fight because of the example of Jesus (v. 13), who did not deny God but made 'the good confession'. We are charged with remaining true and faithful until he returns.

Making the connection between future hopes and current reality can be one of our greatest challenges and very difficult for us to do. We need this greater vision to not only make sense of the here and now and cultivate a better, more Christ-like lifestyle but also because, one day, in Christ, we will give an account of our lives on earth. This is not to frighten us into action but underscore something serious. Our inspiration should be the knowledge that, one day, our strivings will end and unbroken and unending joy will be ours. Paul puts it rather better, asking us to store up treasure 'as a firm foundation for the coming age, so that they may take hold of the life that is truly life' (v. 19).

Prayer

*Strengthen me without and within, gracious God, to fight the good fight
and to take hold of the everlasting life that is your greatest gift,
through your Son Jesus. Amen*

Andrew John

Reflection on 1 Timothy

Timothy, guard what has been entrusted to your care. Turn away from godless chatter and the opposing ideas of what is falsely called knowledge, which some have professed and in so doing have departed from the faith.

Having completed the first letter to Timothy, let us pause to reflect on some key themes before we begin the second. Throughout this letter we have seen Paul's attention to specific pastoral matters concerning welfare (ch. 5), the qualities of leadership (ch. 3) and the way a church orders worship (ch. 2). Some people find these instructions threatening because they come from an age quite different from our own. Rather than get distracted by that, though, we need to hold on to their underlying teaching, which is very important: they show that kingdom values affect everyday matters in the life of the church. The challenge for all pastoral leadership is to translate these principles into terms appropriate to today so they continue to guide us.

Paul is revealed as a preacher, preaching in his writing and exhorting Timothy to the same work (2 Timothy 4). Today, the task of communicating the gospel effectively has never been more important. There are few, if any, inherited narratives to assist or hinder us, but the human condition has not changed. There must be no loss of confidence in the good news, which is God's power to save us. Notice, too, Paul's prophetic ministry. He looks ahead and interprets the times (1 Timothy 4; 2 Timothy 3). This is not gazing into a crystal ball, but is the gift of seeing what God is doing and where challenges lie ahead. A recovery of this gift in the church is overdue because discernment has long been a part of its ministry to the world.

As we turn to 2 Timothy, I hope and pray that it inspires new insights into the God of all grace who has 'brought life and immortality to light' (2 Timothy 1:10).

Prayer

Lord, give us new eyes to see, new ears to hear and new hearts that beat in tune with your own and may the kingdom of your Son Jesus grow in us and flourish in your world, for the praise and glory of your name. Amen

ANDREW JOHN

85

Making it happen

Paul, an apostle of Christ Jesus… to Timothy, my dear son: Grace, mercy and peace from God the Father and Christ Jesus our Lord. I thank God… as night and day I constantly remember you in my prayers… I am reminded of your sincere faith, which first lived in your grandmother Lois and in your mother Eunice and, I am persuaded, now lives in you also. For this reason I remind you to fan into flame the gift of God, which is in you.. For the Spirit God gave us does not make us timid, but gives us power, love and self-discipline.

At the start of this letter, we find similar messages to those in the first letter repeated here, but with new urgency. The strong connection between Paul and Timothy makes it compelling reading and, although there is personal affection, it is principally their shared ministry that inspires much of the letter. Paul's purpose is not to 'touch base' so much as strengthen his friend and junior colleague. He begins with affirmation, acknowledging the faith in Timothy's family (v. 5). This recollection is designed to affirm the continuing commitment of God's faithfulness. By calling to mind God's work in this way, Paul is able to affirm the reality of what God is doing in Timothy.

It is sometimes difficult for us to see God's work in our own lives, but easier to see it in others'. Paul urges Timothy to let God's gift to him burst into life (v. 6). Possibly Timothy lacked confidence (v. 7), which could easily result in timidity and even denial of the faith. Paul's appeal is to the gospel—a gospel that is powerful, but made visible in weakness and suffering (v. 8). This is a profoundly powerful message for us today because a confidence in God, which is neither boastful nor shallow and matched to a willingness to bear and feel the cost of hard choices, stands out from a world where the short cut and short term is prevalent.

Prayer

Lord, thank you for those who have made my faith stronger and walked beside me as fellow disciples. Bless them today and make them a continued source of hope for me. Amen

ANDREW JOHN

2 TIMOTHY 1:13–18 (NIV, ABRIDGED)

Disappointments and deposits

What you heard from me, keep as the pattern of sound teaching, with faith and love in Christ Jesus. Guard the good deposit that was entrusted to you—guard it with the help of the Holy Spirit who lives in us. You know that everyone in the province of Asia has deserted me... May the Lord show mercy to the household of Onesiphorus, because he often refreshed me and was not ashamed of my chains... May the Lord grant that he will find mercy from the Lord... You know very well in how many ways he helped me in Ephesus.

The cost of following Christ fuels much of today's passage and Paul describes some personal trials that accompanied his missionary journeys. Such deeply painful episodes help us to see the humanity of an apostle who seems way ahead of us but actually encountered difficulties, too. Paul's troubles were real and hurt him (v. 15); sometimes in ministry, wounds are inflicted and received and, whatever their cause, they do not heal quickly. Simply acknowledging this preserves us from the kind of gospel in which avoiding hardship is the main attraction.

There is mention of moments of grace along the way, too—blessed Onesiphorus! Scholars are unclear about Paul's prayer for him (v. 18). Had Onesiphorus died, so this is a plea for the salvation of his soul? Some Christians believe so, but this raises many other questions. Was Onesiphorus perhaps in prison and separated from his family, rather than dead? Whatever the situation, the key in today's passage is to understand that faithfulness (v. 13) does not give us licence to avoid hardship. Once again, this can be quite at odds with much contemporary thinking. We should remember Jesus' words, that following him means carrying a cross (Mark 8:34). In both the writings of Paul and the words of Jesus, we see that there is blessedness in sharing in Christ's suffering and it is this that sustains and strengthens us.

Prayer

Lord, when it is easy to complain that life is difficult, help me to draw on Paul's example and see things from the perspective of your suffering, for your name's sake. Amen

ANDREW JOHN

Pictures to inspire

Join with me in suffering, like a good soldier of Christ Jesus. No one serving as a soldier gets entangled in civilian affairs, but rather tries to please his commanding officer. Similarly, anyone who competes as an athlete does not receive the victor's crown except by competing according to the rules. The hardworking farmer should be the first to receive a share of the crops... Here is a trustworthy saying: If we died with him, we will also live with him; if we endure, we will also reign with him. If we disown him, he will also disown us; if we are faithless, he remains faithful, for he cannot disown himself.

Paul uses three pictures to encourage Timothy to faithfulness: the soldier, the athlete and the farmer. The first image reminds us that faith involves an allegiance. As a soldier is required to operate as a soldier, so the Christian must be a disciple. The requirement of serious dedication is reinforced in the next image, with the emphasis less on the effort and training than on the rules. Those who attempt to operate outside the rules are disqualified. Last, the hardworking farmer can share in the profits of his endeavour. Half-hearted investments are not only ineffective but also deny any gain to the investor.

These pictures lead Paul to the poetry of verses 11–13, in which the stages of Christian conversion, perseverance/reward and final judgment are woven together. The radical call to new life lies behind the first line and recalls the early connection of conversion to baptism, but faith also involves following. We are called to endure and persevere rather than deny. If we walk away from God, he walks from us. What of the last line? Some scholars think it repeats the denial, saying that, if we deny Christ, he cannot be other than true to himself and must also deny us. It is equally plausible, though, that a more hopeful point is being made—that, ultimately, God's faithfulness will triumph whatever the human frailty and disobedience involved.

Prayer

Thank you, Lord, for these pictures, which help me root my life more deeply in you. May I do a little more of this today, for Jesus' sake. Amen

Andrew John

Busting the babble

Keep reminding God's people of these things. Warn them before God against quarrelling about words; it is of no value, and only ruins those who listen. Do your best to present yourself to God as one approved, a worker who does not need to be ashamed and who correctly handles the word of truth. Avoid godless chatter, because those who indulge in it will become more and more ungodly... In a large house there are articles not only of gold and silver, but also of wood and clay; some are for special purposes and some for common use. Those who cleanse themselves from the latter will be instruments for special purposes, made holy, useful to the Master.

Here, Paul returns to things he has said elsewhere, but now he gives them new urgency by attaching them to his emphasis on faithful living. Timothy is to present himself as both a faithful worker (v. 15) and work to ensure that others follow suit (v. 14). Whatever may have characterised our living previously need not hinder us in the future because God is able to turn what is unholy into something more beautiful and righteous (vv. 20–21).

There are dangers, however, that must be consciously avoided, lest they damage the individual Christian as well as the church. First, Paul attacks what appears to have been a real problem—irreverent babble (v. 16) and foolish controversies (v. 23). It is true that Christians can be extraordinarily committed to the tiniest details of faith and more passionate about disagreeing over them than many more important matters, such as sharing the gospel or caring for those suffering unjustly. Second, Paul makes the point that such attitudes contain within them something which damages the body of Christ, leading to ungodliness and error (v. 19). Paul is not suggesting that real and important issues of faith are irrelevant; he is, instead, connecting the way in which foolish arguments lead us away from godliness and the truth.

Prayer

Lord of truth and life, give me a greater concern for important matters and help me to avoid what diminishes me and others by words or deeds, for your sake. Amen

Andrew John

89

Always learning, never knowing

Mark this: there will be terrible times in the last days. People will be lovers of themselves, lovers of money, boastful, proud, abusive, disobedient to their parents, ungrateful, unholy, without love, unforgiving, slanderous, without self-control, brutal, not lovers of the good, treacherous, rash, conceited, lovers of pleasure rather than lovers of God—having a form of godliness but denying its power. Have nothing to do with such people... They are... always learning but never able to come to a knowledge of the truth. Just as Jannes and Jambres opposed Moses, so also these teachers oppose the truth... But they will not get very far because... their folly will be clear to everyone.

In today's passage, Paul draws out the full scale of what occupied him in yesterday's verses. His list of godless acts is comprehensive and penetrating and, although his final gloss (v. 9) is important, we should not skirt quickly around his words. Such things are signs that the 'last days' are near and should therefore make us more urgent in choosing Christ.

How should we read this list? Note, first, Paul's use of the word 'lovers' (vv. 2, 4). Rather than lovers of God, he sees a perversion of what might be good and holy. People will become lovers of 'self' and 'pleasure'. You will probably know the story of Narcissus, who supposedly bent down and saw his reflection in a pool of water and fell in love with himself. It is a kind of morality tale about the real dangers of being self-absorbed.

Second, we should notice the futility of searching for meaning and purpose in this way (v. 7). Whatever pleasure is found, it leads nowhere and, ultimately, destroys us. Paul appeals to Exodus 7—9 (v. 8) and the brother magicians (named by later tradition), to show that empty alternatives to the truth of Christ will be exposed as wrong. Paul's aim is to expose the inherent weakness of the godless life he describes and its inability to lead us to the truth, which we know is Christ.

Prayer

Lord, inspire my heart to be captivated by what is good and holy and to make these qualities my enduring pursuit, for the sake of Jesus. Amen

ANDREW JOHN

Written words, living words

You... know all about my teaching, my way of life, my purpose, faith, patience, love, endurance, persecution, sufferings... Yet the Lord rescued me from all of them. In fact, everyone who wants to live a godly life in Christ Jesus will be persecuted, while evildoers and impostors will go from bad to worse, deceiving and being deceived... All Scripture is God-breathed and is useful for teaching, rebuking, correcting and training in righteousness, so that the servant of God may be thoroughly equipped for every good work.

Today, we read one of the great verses in this letter that has given confidence to Christians across the ages (v. 17), but we are also presented with Paul as a source of confidence! We might be startled at the willingness of someone to commend themselves so confidently, but a good bit of our hesitation here is cultural and such reserve is alien to many other cultures. More important, we can miss the point Paul is making—that his own example shows the truth and worth of Christian discipleship (vv. 10–11). Paul's life commends itself in its hardships and is therefore proved to be genuine and authentic. In short, it is Christlike.

The other source of confidence is scripture, which has God's stamp all over it. Some have wanted to translate verse 17 along the lines of 'every scripture inspired by God is profitable for teaching' because they are uneasy about ways in which the Bible has been read and assume that Paul is offering some theory of inspiration. A better reading is the usual 'All scripture is God-breathed' because this was the inherited Jewish understanding and Paul appears to emphasise the trustworthiness of scripture in its totality. That is, it is good for training and correcting to equip the workers of God.

So, there are two great gifts that belong together—the authentic life of God in us and the living word of God in us. How might these gifts embed more completely in our lives?

Prayer
May your word be a lamp to my feet and a light to my path so that, in and through me, something of you might be seen and known, gracious Lord.
Amen

ANDREW JOHN

2 TIMOTHY 4:1–8 (NIV, ABRIDGED)

Towards the end

In the presence of God and of Christ Jesus, who will judge the living and the dead, and in view of his appearing and his kingdom, I give you this charge: preach the word; be prepared in season and out of season; correct, rebuke and encourage—with great patience and careful instruction. For the time will come when people will not put up with sound doctrine... But you, keep your head in all situations, endure hardship... discharge all the duties of your ministry. For I am already being poured out like a drink offering, and the time for my departure is near. I have fought the good fight, I have finished the race, I have kept the faith. Now there is in store for me the crown of righteousness.

As Paul nears the end of his letter, he shares some personal reflections that give us insight into the way in which he understood his service and how he viewed the future. He connects these statements with his continuing concern for Timothy's ministry (vv. 1–2), repeating that a time will come when people will be less receptive to the gospel (vv. 3–4).

In relation to the future, Paul gives us two metaphors: the drink offering and the athlete completing the race. The drink offering refers to the Old Testament pouring of wine in the temple as an act of commitment to God. Paul sees his own life like this–the race has been run, the fight has been fought (v. 7). These emotionally charged verses challenge us to see the all-surpassing importance of Christ. If the future is marked by a sense of fulfilment, it is completed by hope and confidence, which are appropriate to Paul's life and, more importantly, God's grace (v. 8). It is easy to look back at our lives with either regret or nostalgia. Although conscious of the end, Paul's outlook is different: he looks forward to the time when he will be face to face with the one who made him and saved him.

Prayer
Lord, I pray you will help me to view the future with the eyes of faith, not to fear for anything and aim for what is good and holy, for Jesus' sake.
Amen

ANDREW JOHN

2 Timothy 4:9–10, 16–18 (NIV, abridged)

A fitting conclusion

Do your best to come to me quickly, for Demas... has deserted me... At my first defence, no one came to my support, but everyone deserted me. May it not be held against them. But the Lord stood at my side and gave me strength, so that through me the message might be fully proclaimed and all the Gentiles might hear it. And I was delivered from the lion's mouth. The Lord will rescue me from every evil attack and will bring me safely to his heavenly kingdom. To him be glory for ever and ever. Amen.

As we come to our final passage, there are some further practical matters Paul wishes to share with Timothy, but even the smaller details have their own story. Demas, mentioned two other times in the New Testament (Colossians 4:14; Philemon 24), has finally given up and deserted Paul. The trials Paul has endured lead him to place the guilt of his persecutors into God's hands and, at the same time, pray for those who deserted him (2 Timothy 4:16). Among his final remarks, however, we find a confident note on which to end. In all of the difficulties, God is Paul's strength (v. 17) and this hope leads him onwards to the very end (v. 18).

These faith statements commend themselves to us in that casting a glance backwards can help us see the Lord has been a good deal nearer to us and helping us than we may have realised and we need to allow this to lead us forward, whatever our situation. Here, then, is a great encouragement to all who face uncertainty or carry great fears or worries. Here is the gift of faith that tells us to trust God even in the face of pain or death. It is the confidence that comes from knowing Christ will bring us 'safely' home. This is not only a blessed confidence for all God's children, but truly a fitting place to end.

Prayer

Heavenly Father, as I reflect on my life, help me to not live in the past but trust you for the future and know your presence at all times, for Jesus' sake. Amen

ANDREW JOHN

Jesus' wisdom in Luke 13—16

The apostle Paul describes Christ as the power of God and the wisdom of God (1 Corinthians 1:24). Luke shows us how this was lived out by Jesus as he went about God's work on earth. In our readings from his Gospel over the next two weeks, we see Jesus speaking and acting God's power and wisdom as he made his way towards Jerusalem. Many tried to make him turn aside, for it seemed to them utter folly to go to the city where there was so much hostility towards him, but Jesus knew that the proclamation of the gospel in word and deed was not about the 'wisdom of this age' but, rather, 'God's wisdom, secret and hidden, which God decreed before the ages' (1 Corinthians 2:6–7). It is vital that we read Jesus' words to his disciples and his opponents in their context, otherwise we will empty them of their gospel content. When Jesus talked about money, for example, he was warning of life choices that had eternal consequences.

The chapters under consideration in the pages that follow contain some of the hard sayings of Jesus that can make us feel uncomfortable if we have an image of him that is anodyne, but we must take them seriously if we are to hear and respond to the good news correctly. Repentance is a call to turn away from our sinful ways in order to turn towards God's mercy.

People searching for wisdom today usually start with contemporary concerns and values and turn to those who seem to offer ways of living well. These chapters from Luke are concerned with questions of life and death that are as important to us today as they were to his original hearers. Over and over, Jesus uses homely images to lay bare vital truths about God's character and the demands made of those who would be his disciples. As we reflect on these images, we discover more about who God is and just how much he longs for us to know him. Gardening, meals, farming, housekeeping and suchlike provide the basis of parables and straightforward commands about how to gain insight into the wisdom of the kingdom of God.

Liz Hoare

A question of life

At that very time there were some present who told [Jesus] about the Galileans whose blood Pilate had mingled with their sacrifices. He asked them, 'Do you think that because these Galileans suffered in this way they were worse sinners than all other Galileans? No, I tell you; but unless you repent, you will all perish as they did. Or those eighteen who were killed when the tower of Siloam fell on them—do you think that they were worse offenders than all the others living in Jerusalem? No, I tell you; but unless you repent, you will all perish just as they did.'

It is a question often asked when someone suffers: what did he or she do to deserve that? If the Galileans in verse 1 were minding their own business, how much more were the people in Siloam innocent victims of a random incident? Such events confront us daily and we search desperately for explanations. Jesus, himself from Galilee, turns the conversation around and creates an opportunity to urge repentance.

Repetition in the Bible is always there for a good reason. We are to take notice: 'Don't miss this', it is saying. Twice Jesus utters his grave words of warning: 'Unless you repent you will all be destroyed in the same way.' What is he talking about? If his warning that those who refuse to repent will die 'in the same way' refers to the manner of death of the Galileans and the people of Siloam, he is talking about the way that people will die, which was violently.

We have to see this whole passage in the light of the fall of Jerusalem in AD70, for Luke interprets that event as the direct result of its people's refusal to heed Jesus' words and repent and believe in him. We may not be given satisfactory answers to human dilemmas, but it is imperative that we pay attention to human destiny. We are all sinners, we all need to turn to God in repentance and receive his forgiveness (Romans 3:20–26).

Reflection

The call to repentance, though it is addressed specifically to Israel here, is one we need to hear again and again.

LIZ HOARE

Seeking fruit

Then [Jesus] told this parable: 'A man had a fig tree planted in his vineyard; and he came looking for fruit on it and found none. So he said to the gardener, "See here! For three years I have come looking for fruit on this fig tree, and still I find none. Cut it down! Why should it be wasting the soil?" He replied, "Sir, let it alone for one more year, until I dig round it and put manure on it. If it bears fruit next year, well and good; but if not, you can cut it down."'

Good gardeners are patient people. They do not put potatoes in one week and dig them up the next to see what is happening. They are content to wait for nature to move at its own pace. The gardener here is no exception, for, despite three years of disappointment and the costliness of careful cultivation, he is not yet ready to turn his back on this fig tree. He wants to make one last attempt at providing the right conditions and give it the right amount of care and attention to create the best possible conditions for a favourable outcome—a healthy crop of figs.

Whether we see the vineyard owner as God the Father or Jesus, the message is clear: there is a time limit on the invitation to repent and bear the fruit of repentance. Jesus may be alluding to Micah 7:1, where God looks for grapes and figs in the garden of the nation but cannot find any. The image of the fig tree and fruitfulness is a reminder of the importance of producing fruit in our Christian lives (Ephesians 2:8–10; Titus 2:11–14). John the Baptist had already connected repentance with fruit-bearing (Luke 3:8), in that it is a turning around to be reorientated towards a new life, a fruitful one.

Reflection and prayer

Reflect today on the vivid image of the barren tree and imagine what it could be like. Then speak to the Lord about your own life and how fruitful it is at present. As you do so, let the patience and generosity of the gardener's heart encourage you to be honest and hopeful.

LIZ HOARE

God's priorities

Now [Jesus] was teaching in one of the synagogues on the sabbath. And just then there appeared a woman with a spirit that had crippled her for eighteen years. She was bent over and was quite unable to stand up straight. When Jesus saw her, he called her over and said, 'Woman, you are set free from your ailment.' When he laid his hands on her, immediately she stood up straight and began praising God. But the leader of the synagogue… kept saying to the crowd, 'There are six days on which work ought to be done; come on those days and be cured, and not on the sabbath day.' But the Lord answered him and said, 'You hypocrites! Does not each of you on the sabbath untie his ox or his donkey from the manger, and lead it away to give it water? And ought not this woman, a daughter of Abraham… be set free from this bondage on the sabbath day?'

Jesus' wisdom was consistent in both word and deed. He looked at this woman, bent double, perhaps in pain, and saw who she truly was—a daughter of Abraham. The fact that she was a woman and crippled meant that, in those days, she had no worth in the sight of the religious authorities and so they would almost certainly have ignored her. The synagogue leader, who opposed Jesus' healing actions, was a guardian of the rules surrounding what you could and could not do on the sabbath. His argument was that the healing could have waited for another day, but true wisdom is not always to be found in simply keeping to the rules.

Jesus challenged this man in his own terms. How was it acceptable to show compassion for an ass on the sabbath, but not to a human being—in this case a daughter of Abraham? This title conveys promise, dignity, identity and worth—all the things that she had not received to date. Setting the woman free on the sabbath demonstrates the true character of the Lord of the sabbath.

Prayer
Lord, please help me to see people as you see them,
not as society pigeonholes them.

LIZ HOARE

Kingdom qualities

[Jesus] said therefore, 'What is the kingdom of God like? And to what should I compare it? It is like a mustard seed that someone took and sowed in the garden; it grew and became a tree, and the birds of the air made nests in its branches.' And again he said, 'To what should I compare the kingdom of God? It is like yeast that a woman took and mixed in with three measures of flour until all of it was leavened.'

What images come to mind when you try to describe the kingdom of God? Here are two vivid parables describing ordinary everyday occurrences to help us understand what it will be like.

First, a tiny seed planted grows into a huge tree, providing shelter for all the birds. Second, a woman uses yeast to make bread. I enjoy making bread and one of the most satisfying moments is lifting the damp cloth from the resting dough and seeing that it has doubled in size. The amount of flour mentioned here is vast and still a tiny lump of yeast can make it grow as it gradually permeates the whole mixture. It makes no sound, there is no dramatic explosion, but the effect is transformative. Such an apparently simple domestic activity can provide profound insight into the nature of the kingdom of God.

The results are important, too: the tree provides shelter for the birds of the air (and we know that God notices every single sparrow) and bread is a basic staple food that provides nourishment, which is why we pray, 'Give us this day our daily bread' (Matthew 6:11).

The parables are told as explanations in response to the healing that has taken place, which drew such different responses from the crowd and Jesus' opponents. The healing of a single woman, whom no one rated as important, was an instance of Satan being overcome and God's kingdom moving forward. Where do you see tiny seeds being planted for the kingdom in your community?

Reflection and prayer

What surprises you about these two parables? Thank God for your church, however small, and ask him to help you be like the leaven in the flour in your community.

LIZ HOARE

Upside down wisdom

[Jesus] said to them, 'Strive to enter through the narrow door; for many, I tell you, will try to enter and will not be able. When once the owner of the house has got up and shut the door, and you begin to stand outside and to knock at the door, saying, "Lord, open to us", then in reply he will say to you, "I do not know where you come from." Then you will begin to say, "We ate and drank with you, and you taught in our streets." But he will say, "I do not know where you come from; go away from me, all you evildoers!" There will be weeping and gnashing of teeth when you see Abraham and Isaac and Jacob and all the prophets in the kingdom of God, and you yourselves thrown out. Then people will come from east and west, from north and south, and will eat in the kingdom of God. Indeed, some are last who will be first, and some are first who will be last.'

The question of who will be saved is no less interesting now than it was in Jesus' day. Despite Jesus' refusal to give statistics, people have gone on speculating about it and missed the whole point. It is not even enough to say, for example, 'Lord, we were there with you.'

Verses 28 to 30 are a warning to the nation that believed it had a privileged position in God's sight. Its people assumed that they would be first in the queue into the kingdom. So, to hear that there would be others from far away who would sit down and feast with their ancestors Abraham, Isaac and Jacob was shocking.

The final verse above shows the wisdom of Jesus turning human wisdom on its head. His words are meant as good news for those who are shut out, but there is also an unmistakable challenge for everybody who overlooks the radical invitation of Jesus and assumes that all will be well. The interesting academic question 'Will the saved be few?' has turned into a directly personal challenge: 'Will the saved be you?'

Prayer
Lord, help me to keep on trusting in your generous mercy for my salvation.

LIZ HOARE

Wisdom from the farmyard

Some Pharisees came and said to [Jesus], 'Get away from here, for Herod wants to kill you.' He said to them, 'Go and tell that fox for me, "Listen, I am casting out demons and performing cures today and tomorrow, and on the third day I finish my work. Yet today, tomorrow, and the next day I must be on my way, because it is impossible for a prophet to be killed away from Jerusalem." Jerusalem, Jerusalem, the city that kills the prophets and stones those who are sent to it! How often have I desired to gather your children together as a hen gathers her brood under her wings, and you were not willing! See, your house is left to you. And I tell you, you will not see me until the time comes when you say, "Blessed is the one who comes in the name of the Lord."'

I remember my horror when I found my broody hen's chicks lying dead in their run. A fierce storm had prevented them from hearing their mother's urgent cries to shelter with her and they drowned. The striking image in our passage is of the protective mother hen who gathers her young underneath her wings where there is warmth and safety, leads them to good sources of nourishment and fights off threatening foes. Jesus is deliberately developing a picture of God that is rooted in the Old Testament and his hearers would have been familiar with it.

This farmyard picture is especially important in the context of judgement, however, because the mother hen provides shelter from disaster under her wings. The prophet Isaiah referred to the Lord hovering like protective birds over the terrified city of Jerusalem (Isaiah 31:5). If only the people had put their trust in God and not looked to foreign alliances for protection! Would they listen this time, now that God had come in person and demonstrated his loving care in so many ways? Would they listen to Jesus' words of warning and invitation?

Prayer

'He will cover you with his pinions, and under his wings you will find refuge' (Psalm 91:4). With this image in mind, pray about any troubles that you are facing.

LIZ HOARE

Rules again

On one occasion when Jesus was going to the house of a leader of the Pharisees to eat a meal on the sabbath, they were watching him closely. Just then, in front of him, there was a man who had dropsy. And Jesus asked the lawyers and Pharisees, 'Is it lawful to cure people on the sabbath, or not?' But they were silent. So Jesus took him and healed him, and sent him away. Then he said to them, 'If one of you has a child or an ox that has fallen into a well, will you not immediately pull it out on a sabbath day?' And they could not reply to this.

For Luke, healing is a sign of the kingdom and this episode shows the dangers of what could be termed the 'Pharisaic mind'—the tendency to justify oneself through one's ability to keep to the rules as well as placing unbearable burdens on others to do so, too. The Pharisees watched Jesus to see if he could keep to the rules and, at this dinner party, they could put him to the test.

What is sad about the healing of the man is that, by the Pharisees' own standards, this was the right thing to do. In his wisdom, Jesus simply asks them what they would do themselves and, when they are silent, points out that they would rescue a child from a well or even an ox, so why not rescue this man from his distress? We may see the logic of that situation, but are there instances where our own rigid refusal to open up to something new is very costly? The cost here is that the Pharisees cannot see the kingdom breaking in before their very eyes. They are literally speechless in their indignation at being challenged.

All this took place at a meal where Jesus was shown hospitality, but not allowed to exercise his freedom to act as God's Saviour should. The healed man should have been a cause for celebration. Instead, he aroused their hostility.

Prayer

Ask God to open up your expectations of joy and celebration as you see signs of his kingdom breaking into your life and that of your church.

LIZ HOARE

Dinner party etiquette

When [Jesus] noticed how the guests chose the places of honour, he told them a parable. 'When you are invited by someone to a wedding banquet, do not sit down at the place of honour, in case someone more distinguished than you has been invited by your host; and the host who invited both of you may come and say to you, "Give this person your place", and then in disgrace you would start to take the lowest place. But when you are invited, go and sit down at the lowest place, so that when your host comes, he may say to you, "Friend, move up higher"; then you will be honoured in the presence of all who sit at the table with you. For all who exalt themselves will be humbled, and those who humble themselves will be exalted.'

Luke continues to focus on Jesus' meal with the Pharisees to teach more about the nature of the kingdom of God. The fact that he tells us clearly Jesus' words here are a parable means we are to look for a deeper meaning. The wisdom offered here is far more important than how to behave at posh dinner parties! The real point is directed towards those who push themselves forward in God's sight, those who think they are more faithful to his word than everyone else, holier, more zealous.

The Pharisee at whose home Jesus was eating kept the Law scrupulously. Why, he must have asked, did Jesus waste time on the likes of a nobody with dropsy (see yesterday's passage)? 'We know that you are a teacher who has come from God,' admitted Nicodemus on behalf of his Pharisee community (John 3:2). The Pharisees could not stop watching Jesus, but neither could they bring themselves to respond to his message with humility and generosity. God, however, is not bound by our rules and, in his kingdom, it is those who humble themselves before him who are exalted. Mary's song (Luke 1:46–55) echoes down the ages still.

Prayer

*Lord Jesus, thank you that it is by grace we are saved
and made welcome at your table.*

Liz Hoare

Hospitality that challenges

[Jesus] said also to the one who had invited him, 'When you give a luncheon or a dinner, do not invite your friends or your brothers or your relatives or rich neighbours, in case they may invite you in return, and you would be repaid. But when you give a banquet, invite the poor, the crippled, the lame, and the blind. And you will be blessed, because they cannot repay you, for you will be repaid at the resurrection of the righteous.'

Jesus is adamant that the good news is for everyone and God's grace is unrestricted—a theme that emerges strongly in Luke's Gospel. At the start of Jesus' public ministry (4:18), he shows how the gospel is good news for 'the poor'—an all-embracing term for people who recognise their need for God's grace. These are the people specially invited to the heavenly banquet, so they should be given seats at our celebrations rather than those who *expect* an invitation and whom we may be sure will invite us back.

Yet again, the wisdom of Jesus upsets our notions of what is proper and acceptable. This is boundary-crossing hospitality. We may imagine a smart dinner party in an affluent part of town where wine flows and the 'right' people are present in their designer clothes. Is it also true that a simple supper at home with friends is just as problematic because we have surrounded ourselves with people like us who will return the hospitality in an equally cosy fashion? Imagine the same scenes, but with the seats filled by homeless people, drug addicts, those who are unemployed, the unwashed. Who else might we place there and what does that say about God's invitation to his great banquet?

Table fellowship is the starting point for a new kind of society where there are different values, such as non-reciprocal generosity. We may have very real and sensible anxieties about inviting people off the streets into our homes for meals, but we cannot escape the value of the radical nature of Jesus' teaching about who is acceptable in his kingdom.

Prayer

Dear Lord, give me the same kind of generosity towards others
that you have demonstrated in Jesus.

LIZ HOARE

Excuses, excuses

One of the dinner guests, on hearing [Jesus' words], said to him, 'Blessed is anyone who will eat bread in the kingdom of God!' Then Jesus said to him, 'Someone gave a great dinner and invited many. At the time for the dinner he sent his slave to say to those who had been invited, "Come; for everything is ready now." But they all alike began to make excuses. The first said to him, "I have bought a piece of land, and I must go out and see it; please accept my apologies." Another said, "I have bought five yoke of oxen, and I am going to try them out; please accept my apologies." Another said, "I have just been married, and therefore I cannot come."'

By the time you read this, more than a year will have passed since parties were held all over the UK to celebrate the Queen's Diamond Jubilee. Imagine that she gave an enormous banquet at Buckingham Palace, using all the royal silver and her best china. It would include a mouth-watering menu with food most of us only dream of and wine from the royal cellars to match. Imagine all this—and that you have been invited. You would wonder at your good luck and move heaven and earth to clear your diary to be there, surely? Only the most ardent anti-royalist would pass such an opportunity by.

God's hospitality anticipates the messianic banquet in the kingdom of God, as the enthusiastic dinner guest in our passage today realised (v. 15). Sadly, many of those who have been waiting for the kingdom of God to arrive do not like what it proves to be and they turn away. Once again, Jesus uses the image of hospitality as the starting point for understanding a new kind of society. All we have to do is accept the invitation to sit and eat. The host has gone to a great deal of trouble and the banquet is not cancelled when no one turns up, as the story goes on to show (vv. 21–24). In fact, at the end, there is still room.

Prayer

Thank you, Lord Jesus, for your generous invitation to your heavenly banquet. Help us, in turn, to share the good news so that others may join in, too. Amen

LIZ HOARE

Counting the cost

Now large crowds were travelling with [Jesus]; and he turned and said to them, 'Whoever comes to me and does not hate father and mother, wife and children, brothers and sisters, yes, and even life itself, cannot be my disciple. Whoever does not carry the cross and follow me cannot be my disciple. For which of you, intending to build a tower, does not first sit down and estimate the cost, to see whether he has enough to complete it? Otherwise, when he has laid a foundation and is not able to finish, all who see it will begin to ridicule him, saying, "This fellow began to build and was not able to finish."'

The seriousness of following Jesus is unmistakable in this passage, leaving us in no doubt that this is not a lifestyle choice but involves total commitment. The context is important. Large crowds were following Jesus by now and they would have had a variety of motives, including plain curiosity. Jesus was set on his course to Jerusalem and it was dangerous. Would people be prepared to risk everything to go with him?

Are we prepared for the possibility of the costliness of following Jesus, risking our homes and possessions and even our closest relationships? We may not actually be called to do so, but would we, if it came to it? The point of Jesus' words is to compel us to contemplate the implications of following him. There is an urgency about what he says here, that he is laying down an all-or-nothing challenge. It is as relevant today as it was for Jesus' first hearers.

The picture of the tower builder is rather closer to home than is comfortable in the current economic climate. Many such projects lie in the dust, begun when there was optimism and growth, only to have been abandoned in the downturn. In Jerusalem, there was Herod the Great's unfinished temple, soon to be destroyed, as Luke well knew. We cannot see the future, but we need to make sure that we invest in what will last and have counted the cost before we set out.

Prayer

*Lord, may we and all your people live up to the challenge
of a wholehearted discipleship. Amen*

LIZ HOARE

The risk-taking shepherd

Now all the tax collectors and sinners were coming near to listen to him. And the Pharisees and the scribes were grumbling and saying, 'This fellow welcomes sinners and eats with them.' So he told them this parable: 'Which one of you, having a hundred sheep and losing one of them, does not leave the ninety-nine in the wilderness and go after the one that is lost until he finds it? When he has found it, he lays it on his shoulders and rejoices. And when he comes home, he calls together his friends and neighbours, saying to them, "Rejoice with me, for I have found my sheep that was lost." Just so, I tell you, there will be more joy in heaven over one sinner who repents than over ninety-nine righteous people who need no repentance.'

How can this familiar parable challenge our walk with God as much as it did for its first hearers?

The fact is that a decent shepherd would not actually leave 99 sheep alone to search for a lost and possibly dead stray. Remember, however, how Jesus persisted in welcoming the 'wrong' sort of people. He challenged the status quo and the assumptions of the world and, in this parable, he continues to do just that.

God is, in fact, like the shepherd in the parable, for he goes after the 'wrong' people and, when he finds them, there is joy and celebration. Furthermore, note that the sheep does nothing to help the shepherd find it—it is through the efforts of the shepherd that it is restored to the fold. The shepherd puts himself, as well as his flock, at risk by going off to look for the missing sheep. Is this amazing picture—of God himself coming to look for us in our lost state—beginning to grip you afresh?

Jesus is challenging the Pharisees and us to see how things look from God's point of view and get an insight into his compassion and his desire for us to come home to him.

Reflection and prayer

'God makes his love for us clear: while we were still sinners, Christ died for us' (Romans 5:8). Thank God that he searched you out and found you.

LIZ HOARE

A woman's heart

'Or what woman having ten silver coins, if she loses one of them, does not light a lamp, sweep the house, and search carefully until she finds it? When she has found it, she calls together her friends and neighbours, saying, "Rejoice with me, for I have found the coin that I had lost." Just so, I tell you, there is joy in the presence of the angels of God over one sinner who repents.'

The parables of the lost sheep and the lost coin balance a male activity in a pastoral setting with a female activity in a domestic one and this is deliberate on Luke's part. This little parable gives us further insight into the heart of God.

The home was central to the lives of the women of Jesus' day and was a place where a woman could not only be free to invite her female friends but also wield significant power. This woman is someone who has valuable resources that would support her family or possibly her business. When she loses one of her coins, she searches single-mindedly until she finds it. Then, in her joy, she throws a party. We are meant to see a picture of God in this woman, as he searches for the people he has lost.

Jesus appears to have been completely at ease with depicting God as a woman searching and then celebrating with her friends. Doubtless to his hearers, though, it was a shocking image. There are, in fact, a number of instances in Luke's Gospel where women experience deep anguish as they endure loss: Mary lost Jesus at the age of 12 in Jerusalem; the widow of Nain's son had died when Jesus took compassion on her; Jesus compared himself to a mother hen trying to protect her chicks from harm. It is this kind of anguish that we are meant to understand lies in the heart of God, which is why he came to earth in Christ to seek out his lost ones and restore them to himself.

Reflection

Imagine the celebration that took place in the home of this woman and reflect on the fact that your relationship with God gives him similar joy.

LIZ HOARE

Faithful discipleship

'Whoever is faithful in a very little is faithful also in much; and whoever is dishonest in a very little is dishonest also in much. If then you have not been faithful with the dishonest wealth, who will entrust to you the true riches? And if you have not been faithful with what belongs to another, who will give you what is your own? No slave can serve two masters; for a slave will either hate the one and love the other, or be devoted to the one and despise the other. You cannot serve God and wealth.' The Pharisees, who were lovers of money, heard all this, and they ridiculed him. So he said to them, 'You are those who justify yourselves in the sight of others; but God knows your hearts; for what is prized by human beings is an abomination in the sight of God.'

Luke repeatedly warns against the danger of attachment to riches as an obstacle to discipleship. Chapter 16 includes two of Jesus' parables concerning wealth on either side of today's passage. The first of these is addressed to the disciples and the second to the Pharisees, whose hypocrisy is exposed in the passage for today.

Jesus again speaks words of wisdom concerning how to live in the world in such a way that honours God and also keeps us safe from temptation. These verses call us to be faithful. We must choose the right master and serve him faithfully and that will involve being faithful in how we use what wealth has been entrusted to us. The parable at the beginning of the chapter praises a steward's single-minded commitment to his personal survival. There are more important riches to aim for, however, and only by being faithful to God and his values will we gain possession of them.

Surely the Pharisees knew you cannot serve two masters, so why did they laugh at Jesus? Was it that their well-motivated zeal for God had gone horribly wrong and they could not see it? Did they fail to perceive that Jesus' way was the way to true wealth?

Prayer
Lord, you see my heart. Please keep me faithful to you.

LIZ HOARE

Stephen's speech (Acts 7:2–53)

It is good to be able to spend two weeks in August on the speech made by Stephen, the first Christian martyr. As the Church calendar sets his feast day on 26 December, his full story is too easily missed in the post-Christmas haze.

We may simply think of his death as the precursor to Saul's dramatic conversion on the road to Damascus (9:1–19), but, in fact, if we look at his lengthy speech before his accusers, we see a fascinating contrast with Peter's earlier sermon at Pentecost (2:14–35). Whereas Peter shares the gospel message with a series of Old Testament (Hebrew Bible) texts, Stephen retells the story of God's dealings with Israel—from the first call to Abraham to the building of Solomon's temple.

Similar retellings crop up in numerous places in scripture—the book of Deuteronomy, Psalms 105 and 106 (among others), Hebrews 11—considering what God has done in the past to provide encouragement or shape rightful attitudes for the future. Stephen has been accused of 'saying things against this holy place [the temple] and the law' (Acts 6:13) and so, in his defence, he tells this story to show how God has been at work over the centuries, above all through the leadership of Moses. At the same time, God's people have consistently rebelled against him. Most shockingly, Stephen goes on to question the very basis of the temple's founding—was it a divine requirement or an essentially human initiative?

The Greek word *martus*, from which we get the English 'martyr', means 'witness'. This has come to have the primary meaning of one so committed to a cause or truth that they are prepared to die rather than deny it. They willingly renounce the chance of seeing whether or not their cause or truth triumphs but are sustained in their suffering by the hope that their sacrifice will bear fruit, somehow, some day. We have to read beyond Stephen's speech, to Acts 8:1, before we see a hint that his death was not fruitless.

In writing these notes, I have been helped by two commentaries on Acts: Loveday Alexander's *PBC Acts* (BRF, 2006) and David J. Williams' *Acts: New International Biblical Commentary* (Hendrickson, 1995).

Naomi Starkey

Called to hope

And Stephen replied: 'Brothers and fathers, listen to me. The God of glory appeared to our ancestor Abraham when he was in Mesopotamia, before he lived in Haran, and said to him, "Leave your country and your relatives and go to the land that I will show you." Then he left the country of the Chaldeans and settled in Haran. After his father died, God had him move from there to this country in which you are now living. He did not give him any of it as a heritage, not even a foot's length, but promised to give it to him as his possession and to his descendants after him, even though he had no child.'

In the opening words of Stephen's speech, he reminds his audience that the story he tells links directly to the present moment. He appeals to his 'brothers and fathers' as, though they may have been sitting in judgment on him, they are all children of the originally childless Abraham and where they are sitting in in the land promised to their forefather. He is saying that the fact they are gathered there at all speaks of the sovereignty and faithfulness of God.

Throughout his speech, Stephen condenses the original stories to highlight his message. As Loveday Alexander (pp. 58–59) puts it, 'Stephen's potted history emphasises the coming out more than the eventual destination, the letting go of certainties more than the acquisition of new possessions.' Abraham is the starting point, not because his entire life was exemplary (far from it), but because the promises made to him mark the origin of Israel's existence as a people with a special relationship with God.

Abraham is commended in Hebrews 11:10 for his faith: 'He looked forward to the city that has foundations, whose architect and builder is God.' His example reminds us that if we submit our lives in obedience to God, we must be content to play our part—however hidden it may be—in his universal purposes rather than clamour impatiently to see the end of the story.

Prayer

Grant us a breadth of vision, O God, so that we remember you are Lord of all time and space, not just of our own little concerns.

NAOMI STARKEY

Acts 7:6–8 (NRSV)

Called to belong

'And God spoke in these terms, that his descendants would be resident aliens in a country belonging to others, who would enslave them and mistreat them for four hundred years. "But I will judge the nation that they serve," said God, "and after that they shall come out and worship me in this place." Then he gave him the covenant of circumcision. And so Abraham became the father of Isaac and circumcised him on the eighth day; and Isaac became the father of Jacob, and Jacob of the twelve patriarchs.'

It comes as a shock to hear that God's promise to Abraham includes the 400 years of suffering and slavery endured by the Israelites in Egypt. The point is, however, not that God wilfully inflicts pain to serve a greater good but that he is omnipotent, despite any indication to the contrary. The warning of suffering is tempered by a promise of judgment on the tyrant nation of Egypt, although so many would have died long before that judgment would come to pass.

Interestingly, the exodus is presented not as an 'escape to the true homeland' but 'being set free to worship'. This sentiment echoes Zechariah's song (itself a mini-retelling of the God–Israel story) at the circumcision of John the Baptist, where he speaks of 'we, being rescued from the hands of our enemies, might serve [the Lord God] without fear, in holiness and righteousness before him all our days' (Luke 1:74–75). The fundamental point of the covenant is not so much possession of the land as the relationship with God that the land symbolises.

God's disclosure to Abraham concludes here with 'the covenant of circumcision'. This was the sign of belonging for the people of God (for the men, anyway) and Stephen's words are a reminder that this sign predated both the Law given to Moses and the building of the temple— the two things he has been accused of denigrating. He is perhaps hinting at what his accusers fail to perceive: God is greater than they know and his agenda encompasses more than they can possibly understand.

Reflection

What do you think should be the sign of belonging
to the people of God today?

NAOMI STARKEY

Called far from home

'The patriarchs, jealous of Joseph, sold him into Egypt; but God was with him, and rescued him from all his afflictions, and enabled him to win favour and to show wisdom when he stood before Pharaoh, king of Egypt, who appointed him ruler over Egypt and over all his household. Now there came a famine throughout Egypt and Canaan, and great suffering, and our ancestors could find no food. But when Jacob heard that there was grain in Egypt, he sent our ancestors there on their first visit. On the second visit Joseph made himself known to his brothers, and Joseph's family became known to Pharaoh.'

Like Daniel and Esther after him, Joseph ends up prospering in exile. Thanks to the sovereign workings of God, he is the right person in the right place at the right time, blessed with wisdom not only to help his own people but also to benefit the community that, for him, is one far from home. A key realisation to come out of the years of Jewish exile in Babylon was that God was not a local deity, limited to a specific territory or sacred location: his authority extended to the ends of the earth.

Joseph's experiences are also a reminder that the patriarchal family was often characterised by rivalry, bitter in-fighting and even violence: 'Stephen reminds his audience that the history of God's people is a history of jealousy and rejection within the family' (Alexander, p. 59). Such, too, was the experience of Jesus, who commented ruefully, 'Prophets are not without honour, except in their home town, and among their own kin, and in their own house' (Mark 6:4). We should remember that Stephen is speaking a relatively short time after Jesus was rejected by his own people—a rejection that led to his violent death. The audience would have been more than a little sensitive to any suggestion that a pattern might be discernible here.

Reflection

'No weapon that is fashioned against you shall prosper, and you shall confute every tongue that rises against you in judgement. This is the heritage of the servants of the Lord and their vindication from me, says the Lord' (Isaiah 54:17).

NAOMI STARKEY

Grave errors?

'Then Joseph sent and invited his father Jacob and all his relatives to come to him, seventy-five in all; so Jacob went down to Egypt. He himself died there as well as our ancestors, and their bodies were brought back to Shechem and laid in the tomb that Abraham had bought for a sum of silver from the sons of Hamor in Shechem.'

At this point, we may pause in puzzlement. If Stephen is summarising the sweep of Jewish history in the closing moments of his life, why so much detail about who was buried where? Also, commentators point out that his narrative seems to confuse two burial stories. Genesis 50:13 says that Jacob was buried on the land bought by Abraham at Hebron (see 23:15–19); Joshua 24:32 tells us that Joseph's bones were brought from Egypt for burial at Shechem, on land bought by Jacob (Genesis 33:19); the Old Testament does not mention where his brothers were buried.

The thought that the Bible contains factual inaccuracies may be very troubling for some, but it is undeniable. Of course it is the inspired word of God, but it was written down by humans (and, here, spoken by a human) and humans sometimes make mistakes or present information in a less than straightforward way! This does not detract in any way from the overall authority of scripture and admitting that there is the occasional error need not diminish our reverence for the text and the truths that it contains.

As to why Stephen should include details about these graves, we can surely understand this if we think of the astonishing rise in the popularity of family history research that has occurred in recent years. Churches constantly field calls from those asking about long ago baptisms, weddings and funerals and whether or not graves can be visited. People want to know about their roots, to affirm 'this is where I come from', even 'this is where part of me belongs'. In death, so Stephen tells us, the patriarchs were brought back to rest in the land given them by God. So, these details matter because belonging matters.

Prayer

O Lord God, thank you for your holy scriptures. Help us to read them with clear eyes, reverence and willingness to receive your word to us each day.

NAOMI STARKEY

Beautiful before God

'But as the time drew near for the fulfilment of the promise that God had made to Abraham, our people in Egypt increased and multiplied until another king who had not known Joseph ruled over Egypt. He dealt craftily with our race and forced our ancestors to abandon their infants so that they would die. At this time Moses was born, and he was beautiful before God. For three months he was brought up in his father's house; and when he was abandoned, Pharaoh's daughter adopted him and brought him up as her own son. So Moses was instructed in all the wisdom of the Egyptians and was powerful in his words and deeds.'

The lovely phrase used as today's title is how the infant Moses is portrayed in Stephen's speech. Exodus 2:2 talks of him as a 'fine baby' (I also like the KJV's 'goodly child'), but the particularly poetic choice of words here is characteristic of the generally heightened picture of Moses that Stephen presents. It is interesting to read of him as 'powerful in his words and deeds' because, in Exodus 4:10, Moses says that he is 'slow of speech and slow of tongue', but perhaps we should allow him some modesty in his description of himself!

Why does he present Moses in this way? We should remember the context for this speech. Stephen has been accused of rejecting the Law that God gave to Israel through Moses and so, by extension, rejecting Moses himself. In his retelling of Moses' life, he shows that, on the contrary, he fully endorses his place as the greatest figure in Israel's history.

The bigger story is coming to its first climax, with the promise to Abraham and the move to Egypt leading to a crisis when genocide looks to be the unavoidable fate of God's people. At such a time of danger, God chooses a mere baby who will grow up—blessed with heavenly wisdom, strength and courage—to be a saviour. There are clear parallels with the life of Jesus, but they are tactfully implicit so as not to undermine Moses. They are mere echoes but ones that the perceptive hearer will notice and understand.

Prayer

Thank you, Lord God, that we are all beautiful in your eyes.

NAOMI STARKEY

Mishearing the call

'When [Moses] was forty years old, it came into his heart to visit his relatives, the Israelites. When he saw one of them being wronged, he... avenged him by striking down the Egyptian. He supposed that his kinsfolk would understand that God through him was rescuing them, but they did not understand. The next day he came to some of them as they were quarrelling and tried to reconcile them, saying, "Men, you are brothers; why do you wrong each other?" But the man who was wronging his neighbour pushed Moses aside, saying, "Who made you a ruler and a judge over us? Do you want to kill me as you killed the Egyptian yesterday?" When he heard this, Moses fled and became a resident alien in the land of Midian. There he became the father of two sons.'

We are told that Moses' desire to reconnect with his relatives 'came into his heart', suggesting that it was a work of God rather than his own instinct. The call to serve and save comes as he reaches the age of 40 (although the Old Testament offers no evidence for this figure). What happens, though, is that he misunderstands how the call should work out in practice. Living in an oppressive society, where slavery and violence are part of everyday life, means that Moses' automatic response to conflict is one of violence.

The story shows the central importance for any would-be servant of God of cultivating attitudes of patience, humility and obedience. If we simply stride out—or hit out—in our strength, powered by our own assumptions about the 'right thing to do', we will probably end up in a mess, later if not sooner. Praying faithfully and expectantly for a situation or person involves bringing our concerns and requests into God's loving presence and waiting, in silence, for his response, which takes much longer and may come in a very different way from what we expect.

Reflection

All of a sudden we just know: *prayer is a conversation in which God's word has the initiative and we, for the moment, can be nothing more than listeners.*

Hans Urs von Balthasar, *Prayer* (Ignatius Press, 1986)

NAOMI STARKEY

A voice in the desert

'Now when forty years had passed, an angel appeared to [Moses] in the wilderness of Mount Sinai, in the flame of a burning bush. When Moses saw it, he was amazed at the sight; and as he approached to look, there came the voice of the Lord: "I am the God of your ancestors, the God of Abraham, Isaac and Jacob." Moses began to tremble and did not dare to look. Then the Lord said to him, "Take off the sandals from your feet, for the place where you are standing is holy ground. I have surely seen the mistreatment of my people who are in Egypt and have heard their groaning, and I have come down to rescue them. Come now, I will send you to Egypt."'

Moses had to turn his back on his comfortable upbringing among the Egyptian ruling class in order to discern God's call correctly. He ends up spending years with the desert-dwelling Midianites, even marrying and raising a family there. Such 'wilderness time' can seem very daunting, when we find ourselves far from familiar routines and landmarks, and we may worry that we have lost our bearings altogether. Perhaps that is what needs to happen, though, for us to begin to work out who we really are and what we ought to do with our lives—and it is only then that we can begin to tune into the gentle whisper of God.

Just as Joseph knew the Lord's presence with him in prison in Egypt, so now Moses hears God at an apparently random site in the barren hills—one that is about as different as imaginable from the grand monuments of the Nile valley. That inauspicious place becomes holy ground, as he realises that he is actually in the presence of God. Finally, Moses understands who is calling him, where he is being called to and what his task will be—a moment as pivotal as the original call to Abraham.

Reflection

'We are fallen in mostly broken pieces… but the wild can still return us to ourselves' (Robert Macfarlane, The Wild Places, *Granta*, 2007). *Where in your life are the 'wild places' where you can pause to be open to God?*

NAOMI STARKEY

Despised and rejected

'It was this Moses whom [the people] rejected when they said, "Who made you a ruler and a judge?" and whom God now sent as both ruler and liberator through the angel who appeared to him in the bush. He led them out, having performed wonders and signs in Egypt, at the Red Sea, and in the wilderness for forty years.'

Stephen's speech changes here from story to statements about Moses. The original Greek text uses the phrase 'this one' (*houtos*) five times in vv. 35–38, underlining the point that it was this very same Moses who was sent by God as a saviour, but was rejected by those he came to save. As already mentioned, Stephen has been accused of rejecting Moses, but here he spells out that, in fact, shockingly, the Israelites did just that. The parallels with what happened to Jesus are now unmistakable.

Moses was rejected (as was Jesus) despite the 'wonders and signs' he did, not only in Egypt but also for decades after in the desert. We may be tempted to assume that a Church characterised by such 'wonders and signs' would pull in the punters effortlessly, but history shows that miracles do not automatically generate Christian disciples. They can certainly do so, but, as often as not, once people receive the answer to prayer that they have sought, they go on their way, perhaps without even so much as a 'thank you' to the God who has touched their lives. It happened to Jesus (Luke 17:11–19).

When we look at Jesus' ministry, we see that his primary purpose was not to be a wonderworker but draw people into that intimate relationship with God that he enjoyed. Luke 8:2–3 talks of Jesus' women followers, including Mary Magdalene, being those he had healed in various ways. They received a wonderful gift but they also went on to know the giver of that gift, the source of such love and grace.

Reflection

'He came to what was his own, and his own people did not accept him. But to all who received him, who believed in his name, he gave power to become children of God' (John 1:11–12).

NAOMI STARKEY

The prophet to come

'This is the Moses who said to the Israelites, "God will raise up a prophet for you from your own people as he raised me up." He is the one who was in the congregation in the wilderness with the angel who spoke to him at Mount Sinai, and with our ancestors; and he received living oracles to give to us.'

Stephen continues in accusatory tones to describe the Israelites' attitude to 'this Moses'. Here he uses a quotation from Deuteronomy 18:15, which records Moses foretelling the coming of another future prophet, one 'raised up' as he was. Yet again, he does not in any way deny the towering significance of Moses but emphasises how he pointed forwards to the coming of Jesus. Also, while Moses brought 'living oracles', Jesus not only brought words of life but also, literally, embodied the eternal life of God's kingdom.

The word translated as 'congregation' is the Greek *ecclesia*, from which we get 'ecclesiastical' (and the French *église* and Welsh *eglwys*). Interestingly, *ecclesia* was the usual term for the community of Israel in the Septuagint (the Greek translation of the Old Testament), which is what Stephen quotes. The word did not necessarily have any particular faith-related overtones at that time and so can serve to remind us that, in essence, the *ecclesia*/church is a community of people rather than a building or authority structure. Looking back at the past with clear eyes is vital for making sense of the present time. We may think that we know what happened 'back then' and how events or people influenced a situation today, but, in fact, perhaps we need to be prepared to reassess our assumptions in the light of new evidence or fresh developments.

Stephen's speech is starting to build to its climax, when his audience will be left with the excruciatingly uncomfortable message that they are the ones who are in the wrong, as their ancestors were before them. The accused is turning the tables on his accusers—a tactic unlikely to bring about a happy ending.

Prayer

O God, may we not be so absorbed with what we think we know that we fail to listen to what you would teach us.

Naomi Starkey

Rebellion

'Our ancestors were unwilling to obey [Moses]; instead, they pushed him aside, and in their hearts they turned back to Egypt, saying to Aaron, "Make gods for us who will lead the way for us; as for this Moses who led us out from the land of Egypt, we do not know what has happened to him." At that time they made a calf, offered a sacrifice to the idol, and revelled in the works of their hands.'

The focus now shifts from Moses to the rebellious people, specifically the appalling incident of the golden calf (Exodus 32). They forget that it was not simply Moses who led them from captivity but Moses acting as the obedient servant of the Lord God, hence their request to Aaron for 'gods… who will lead the way for us' (Acts 7:40). They mentally 'turn back to Egypt', yearning for the place of bitter suffering and enslavement, and literally turn their gaze away from the true God to an idol, 'the works of their hands'. In the final stage of his speech, Stephen links this theme of idolatry to the building of the temple.

It is easy to reflect on this episode with smugness, as if we would never act so stupidly. Right after the inexpressibly solemn time of covenant-making at Sinai, after the smoke, thunder and stone tablets, the Israelites smash it all to pieces. How could they?

We may ask similar questions if we see somebody we know or a figure in the media spotlight losing reputation, relationships, career or whatever as the consequence of actions that we struggle to comprehend. Susan Howatch's popular 'Starbridge' series of novels followed the tangled histories of a number of clerics whose inner turmoil led to painful conflict with their public, professional personas. For me, the power of the novels lay in the way that she sensitively unravelled the complexities of a character's heart and showed how even those in the worst messes could eventually find a path towards healing and wholeness. Even the most broken could hope for the blessing of godly wisdom, if they went in search of it.

Prayer

Holy, ever-loving God, enlarge our hearts to encompass more of your mercy.

NAOMI STARKEY

Relationship unravelling

'But God turned away from them and handed them over to worship the host of heaven, as it is written in the book of the prophets: "Did you offer to me slain victims and sacrifices for forty years in the wilderness, O house of Israel? No; you took along the tent of Moloch, and the star of your god Rephan, the images that you made to worship; so I will remove you beyond Babylon."'

What devastating words: 'God turned away from them' (v. 42). Remember that, at this point in the narrative, we are still with the Israelites in the wilderness, when the Law was given, the tabernacle made and the covenant established with all the people (rather than one individual, as in the past). This historic time of intimacy—as it were, the honeymoon of God with his chosen people—is here shown to be the point where that relationship began to unravel, leading eventually to the catastrophe of exile in Babylon. Yes, Israel offered sacrifices in the wilderness, but to the wrong gods, the 'host of heaven' (see also Jeremiah 8:2, Zephaniah 1:5).

The quote from 'the book of the prophets' is Amos 5:25–27, the Hebrew of which the Greek translators of the Septuagint struggled to understand 600 years after they were written. Nobody knows what 'Rephan' is, for example, and where Amos spoke of being removed to 'Damascus', the name was updated to Babylon in the Septuagint, in the light of what actually happened. The end result was in keeping with the eighth-century BC text, while differing in some of its vocabulary.

Many churches, Christian organisations and festivals look back to a 'golden age' when every seat was taken, every ticket booked, donations flowed and vision was keen. Strangely, the 'golden age' often corresponds to the youth of those looking back! Remembering with thanksgiving is important, but being prepared to move into the future is essential, not least because the future comes, whether we are ready or not.

Prayer

Faithful God, thank you for all that you have done for us in years past. Give us courage and confidence so that we can embrace all that you would do for us in years to come.

Naomi Starkey

Listening matters

'Our ancestors had the tent of testimony in the wilderness, as God directed when he spoke to Moses, ordering him to make it according to the pattern he had seen. Our ancestors in turn brought it in with Joshua when they dispossessed the nations that God drove out before our ancestors. And it was there until the time of David, who found favour with God and asked that he might find a dwelling-place for the house of Jacob.'

Having spent a while on the story of Moses, Stephen now hurries on from a tent in the wilderness to a temple. He has emphasised Moses as a forerunner of Jesus, but the temple is another matter. God had directed the making of the tent whereas Stephen wants to show that the building of the temple was a human initiative, albeit one of David's, the hero warrior king 'who found favour with God'. If we are puzzled by the reference to a 'dwelling-place for the house of Jacob' (v. 46), note that a variant reading for this verse is 'for the God of Jacob'.

However close we may feel to God, however strong in faith, however insightful, we can start to assume that we know best. Instead of humbly laying out our plans in prayer and waiting patiently for assurance (whether from others or in the quiet of our own hearts) we can be convinced that we have chosen the correct course of action and may press on, only to realise afterwards we did not start in the right place, at the right time or with the right people.

I once heard of a wealthy Western congregation that insisted on supporting an African church leader by donating a luxurious three-piece suite for his house. The suite ended up languishing in a customs shed, due to incorrect paperwork, the soft cushions gently rotting in the tropical humidity. The urge to do something, to show compassion, concern and solidarity, was laudable, but it had to be paired with common sense and the willingness to listen—to God and also to the situation and the people concerned.

Reflection

'For wisdom is better than jewels, and all that you may desire cannot compare with her' (Proverbs 8:11).

Naomi Starkey

Sacred space, living God

'But it was Solomon who built a house for him. Yet the Most High does not dwell in houses made by human hands; as the prophet says, "Heaven is my throne, and the earth is my footstool. What kind of house will you build for me, says the Lord, or what is the place of my rest? Did not my hand make all these things?"'

Stephen was not denying that God could be found in the temple; he wanted to emphasise that the presence of God was not limited to the temple, as the quote from Isaiah (66:1–2) makes clear. The temple was a sacred space, but it was still 'made with human hands' (v. 48)—as was the golden calf. Like the golden statue, the problem lay not with the created object in itself but with the attitude of the people that subsequently developed. What should have been a means to an end (encountering the living God) became the end in itself (being custodians of the temple).

Picking up on a point in Monday's notes, we should remind ourselves, from time to time, that our churches are more than the sum of their buildings. Worshipping in a beautifully maintained, historic setting can be a wonderfully enriching experience, but too many congregations find the upkeep of buildings to be a major and depressing drain on their time and money. There is no doubt, though, that for arguably a majority of non-attenders, a church building says 'this is where you can come in search of God'. The negative witness of a closed and decaying church, with an overgrown churchyard and 'For Sale' sign outside, should not be underestimated.

There are no easy answers—there seldom are—and the missional challenge remains one of finding the balance between caring for the bricks and mortar and not becoming so devoted to their well-being that we forget that the fundamental point of the building is as a gathering place for the people.

Reflection
'How lovely is your dwelling-place, O Lord of hosts! My soul longs, indeed it faints for the courts of the Lord; my heart and my flesh sing for joy to the living God' (Psalm 84:1–2).

NAOMI STARKEY

The end

'You stiff-necked people, uncircumcised in heart and ears, you are for ever opposing the Holy Spirit, just as your ancestors used to do. Which of the prophets did your ancestors not persecute? They killed those who foretold the coming of the Righteous One, and now you have become his betrayers and murderers. You are the ones that received the law as ordained by angels, and yet you have not kept it.'

Finally, the speech reaches boiling point. Stephen's words are as scalding as some of Jesus' diatribes against the Pharisees (Matthew 23:16–36). Generation after generation of God's people had completely failed to recognise the Holy Spirit of God at work. They were 'uncircumcised in heart and ears' (Acts 7:51), keeping the letter of the Law of Moses but not honouring the relationship that the Law represented. They were blessed with the most privileged status but chose to go their own way.

Commentators stress the importance of reading Stephen's words here as part of an ongoing contemporary disagreement about the interpretation of scripture rather than in any way 'Christians attacking Jews'. The early years of the Church were full of pain over the difference in understanding between the various groups, differences that finally led to permanent division. The subsequent, deeply shameful history of anti-Semitism means that such texts have to be read and preached with great care and sensitivity.

As his speech concludes, Stephen's hearers are so beside themselves with rage that they drag him away for summary execution (vv. 54–60). What is our reaction when faced with unpalatable, even harsh truths about ourselves? Do we cover our ears and shout louder than the prophetic voice (v. 57) or do we take a deep breath and calm our angrily pounding heart to listen to what we need to hear? Perhaps, instead, we are the ones who know that we have an unpalatable truth to convey to an unwilling or even hostile audience—in which case, we can pray for the courage of one such as Stephen.

Prayer

Thank you, Lord, for the witness of your servant Stephen. We commend to your care all those who face suffering and even death for serving you.

NAOMI STARKEY

Aidan, Cuthbert and Lindisfarne

'On Aidan's arrival, the king appointed the island of Lindisfarne to be his see at his own request. As the tide ebbs and flows, this place is surrounded by sea twice a day like an island, and twice a day the sand dries and joins it to the mainland' (Bede, *Ecclesiastical History of the English People* [EH], Penguin, 1990, p. 147).

Despite changes to our coastline, these words of Bede give a description of the tidal island of Lindisfarne that is as accurate today as it was when it was written nearly 1400 years ago. About a mile off the coast, a few miles south of the present-day Scottish border, the island has a turbulent history, but is now a place of wild, windswept beauty. It is home to wild creatures and sea birds and, in one tiny corner, a community whose families can trace their island roots back centuries.

Archaeological remains indicate that there has been a human presence on the island since prehistoric times, but our concern lies with the arrival of Aidan, Irish-born monk of Iona, in 635. The church he founded on Lindisfarne became the mother church of Northumbria and the seedbed for the growth of Christianity throughout the northern kingdoms of England. The effect was dramatic and far-reaching: 'Here was fostered a place of worship, both simple and profound, that lives on in the annals of the spirit. Here was a great school of religious discipline, an inspired power-house of culture and learning, a seminary of the soul whose missionary graduates would carry the torch of Christianity far afield over Britain and the Continent' (Magnus Magnusson, *Lindisfarne*, The History Press, 2008, pp. 1–2). The spiritual legacy of that work continues today through the witness of the island's parish and Christian community. Thousands of pilgrims visit each year, most by way of the modern tarmac causeway, but some still approach barefoot, following the ancient pilgrim route across the sands at low tide.

In the eleventh century, Lindisfarne was given the additional name of Holy Island, on account of the Celtic saints who lived and worked there. Over the next fortnight, we shall be looking at two of those saints in particular—Aidan and Cuthbert. The light that illumined those early centuries for the northern kingdoms shines still, and we are offered the gift of their spiritual legacy.

Barbara Mosse

Lift high the cross

After the death of Moses... the Lord spoke to Joshua... saying,
'My servant Moses is dead. Now proceed to cross the Jordan, you
and all this people, into the land that I am giving to them... Only
be strong and very courageous, being careful to act in accordance
with all the law that my servant Moses commanded you... Be
strong and courageous; do not be frightened or dismayed, for the
Lord your God is with you wherever you go.'

Joshua emerges at the dawn of a new era: Moses has died and the
Israelites stand on the threshold of the promised land. Joshua is the
man commissioned by God to lead the people into Canaan, to conquer
it and distribute the land under the Law of Moses. Perhaps, like Moses
(Exodus 4:1–5) and, later, Jeremiah (1:6–8), Joshua did not believe that
he was equal to the task, as God exhorts him twice to be strong and
courageous, 'for the Lord your God is with you wherever you go' (v. 9).

Britain at the time we are considering was a turbulent and unsettled
island, a patchwork of warring tribes and kingdoms. A little time before
Aidan arrived on Lindisfarne, Bede tells us of Oswald—the deeply committed Christian king of Northumbria who had grown up in exile on
Iona. Bede describes him as 'a man beloved of God' (*EH*, p. 144) who,
before meeting the pagan Cadwallon of Gwynedd in battle, set up a
wooden cross in the ground and rallied his troops around it: 'Let us all
kneel together, and ask the true and living God Almighty... to protect
us from the arrogant savagery of our enemies, since He knows that we
fight in a just cause to save our nation' (*EH*, p. 144). The site of the
battle became known as Heavenfield and, as with Joshua, the resound-
ing victory was credited to the presence and protection of God. It paved
the way for the subsequent introduction of Christianity to Northumbria
and the spread of the faith far beyond its borders.

Reflection

*How can we look beyond the limited boundaries of local or national events
to discern the God of the ages who transcends the ebb and flow of all
historical and political movements?*

BARBARA MOSSE

Like a lamb among wolves

After this the Lord appointed seventy(-two) others and sent them on ahead of him... He said to them, 'The harvest is plentiful, but the labourers are few; therefore ask the Lord of the harvest to send out labourers into his harvest. Go on your way. See, I am sending you out like lambs into the midst of wolves. Carry no purse, no bag, no sandals; and greet no one on the road.'

Bede records that when King Oswald asked the community on Iona to send a bishop to teach the faith to his people, Aidan was not the original choice. The first man got nowhere and his attempt ended in failure. Too stern and inflexible, he had returned to Iona claiming that the Northumbrians 'were an ungovernable people of an obstinate and barbarous temperament' (*EH*, p. 151). Aidan remonstrated gently with the returning monk and offered constructive advice on alternative ways in which the task could be addressed. Predictably, the community then decided that Aidan was the ideal person for the job!

The situation Aidan faced was daunting and so he went, under obedience, 'like a lamb amidst the wolves'. This story also poses present-day disciples a challenge, however. It is all too easy for us to think that mission is something relating only to those who are specially 'called'. We may find ourselves slipping into a 'here am I—send him or her' mentality. Jesus may have only called the Twelve to form the inner core of his discipleship group, but our reading today from Luke makes it quite clear that Jesus' call to mission extended far beyond just them.

Commentaries give numerous speculative reasons for the number 70 (or 72 in some manuscripts, v. 1), but the most likely interpretation seems to be that it refers to the biblical number of the nations, as listed in Genesis 10. If this is correct, then the task of mission seems intended to be part of the call of each and every disciple, not just a chosen few.

Reflection

What form does the mission of the Church take in your local area? In what ways may God be inviting you to be a part of it?

BARBARA MOSSE

The handing on of the light

[Jesus said] 'You are the light of the world. A city built on a hill cannot be hidden. No one after lighting a lamp puts it under the bushel basket, but on the lampstand, and it gives light to all in the house. In the same way, let your light shine before others, so that they may see your good works and give glory to your Father in heaven.'

In the churchyard on Lindisfarne stands an imposing statue of Aidan. The figure is gaunt and austere, staring into the distance with a gaze of focused intensity. In his right hand he carries a bishop's crook and, in his left, he holds aloft a flaming torch. The setting is dramatic as, bounded by the churchyard wall and flanked by trees, the saint's silhouette stands dramatically outlined against the immense and ever-changing skyscape beyond. The statue has a compelling power and has been much photographed. It presents a potent image of a saint called to bring the light of Christ to the pagan darkness of the northern kingdoms.

The light of Christ, as portrayed, particularly in John's Gospel, is an image both ancient and familiar (John 1:9; 9:5; 12:46). In the example here from Matthew, however, there is a twist: it is the disciples, not Jesus himself, whom he refers to as 'the light of the world' (5:14). Jesus' words offer much encouragement to the present-day as well as the early disciple: we are not to strive to be Christ's light in the world—we *are* Christ's light in the world, simply by virtue of our commitment to him.

This reassurance brings a challenge and a commission. Our light is not to be hidden, but placed 'on the lampstand' (v. 15), where it will give light to all around. Disciples are to let their light shine before others, so that God's love and goodness may be glorified (v. 16). Reflecting the spirit of Aidan, we are called to radiate the light of God to the world around us with courage and humility.

Reflection

As a disciple of Christ, what could being 'the light of the world' mean for you and the community in which you live?

BARBARA MOSSE

Partners in mission

Paul went on also to Derbe and to Lystra, where there was a disciple named Timothy... He was well spoken of by the believers in Lystra and Iconium. Paul wanted Timothy to accompany him... As they went from town to town, they delivered to them for observance the decisions that had been reached by the apostles and elders who were in Jerusalem. So the churches were strengthened in the faith and increased in numbers daily.

After Paul's sharp disagreement with Barnabas (Acts 15:36–39), he is urgently in need of another co-worker and travelling companion. At Lystra, Timothy comes to Paul's attention as he is strongly recommended and well spoken of by the believers in both Lystra and Iconium (16:2). Paul was well aware that, as the infant church grew, others were needed to share in the work of teaching and encouragement. In sending his disciples out in pairs to do the work of mission, Jesus himself established the principle of sharing both the work and the responsibilities.

There is an intriguing example of similar cooperation in mission in the life of Aidan. As an Irishman, he had arrived in Northumbria with very little grasp of the English language. King Oswald, as a result of his prolonged exile as a boy and young man, was fluent in the Irish tongue. So, when Aidan travelled round the Northumbrian kingdom, Oswald would accompany him, translating Aidan's teaching and 'interpreting the word of God to his [Oswald's] ealdormen and thegns' (EH, p. 147).

In both pairings, the characteristics and traits of each person complete and complement the other. Paul, with his unimpeachable Jewish background, badly needed the Greek/Jewish mix that was Timothy's family inheritance as the church grew and expanded into new territories. As an Irishman with only limited English, Aidan needed both the commitment and the linguistic ability of Oswald if his mission to the Northumbrians was to bear any kind of fruit.

Reflection

'Two are better than one, because they have a good reward for their toil. For if they fail, one will lift up the other; but woe to one who is alone and falls and does not have another to help' (Ecclesiastes 4:9–10).

BARBARA MOSSE

The common touch

Then Levi gave a great banquet for [Jesus] in his house; and there was a large crowd of tax-collectors and others sitting at the table with them. The Pharisees and their scribes were complaining to his disciples, saying, 'Why do you eat and drink with tax-collectors and sinners?' Jesus answered, 'Those who are well have no need of a physician, but those who are sick; I have come to call not the righteous but sinners to repentance.'

Meals seem to be especially prominent in Luke: somebody once observed that, in this Gospel, Jesus seems to be virtually always on his way either to or from a meal, generally in the company of those the religious establishment deemed to be outcasts or undesirables. Tax collectors were particularly scorned as they were generally not native to the area in which they worked and the collusion of many with the Roman authorities meant they were despised and mistrusted. The Pharisees regarded such people as ceremonially unclean, both on account of their continual contact with Gentiles and their need to work on the sabbath, so Jesus' insistence on associating with them posed a continual threat.

We see in Aidan, too, a similar disregard for society's and religion's rules of hierarchy and association. Bede states that Aidan continually gave away to the poor the gifts he received from the rich. On one occasion, the gift was a fine, richly adorned horse, given to him by the king. The intention was that Aidan would be able to travel round his vast diocese in greater comfort, but he gave the horse away to the first beggar he met. Bede stresses that Aidan's preference, whether in town or country, was to travel on foot, 'and whatever people he met on his walks, whether high or low, he stopped and spoke to them' (*EH*, p. 150). King Oswald followed his example and 'at once ordered his own food to be taken out to the poor, and the silver dish to be broken up and distributed among them' (*EH*, p. 152).

Reflection

Jesus modelled a life of discipleship in association with outcasts rather than separation from them. How effectively has the church taken up his teaching?

BARBARA MOSSE

Without fear or favour

Jesus was going to the house of a leader of the Pharisees to eat a meal... When he noticed how the guests chose the places of honour, he told them a parable. 'When you are invited by someone to a wedding banquet, do not sit down at the place of honour, in case someone more distinguished than you has been invited by your host... But when you are invited, go and sit down at the lowest place, so that when your host comes, he may say to you, "Friend, move up higher."... He said also to the one who had invited him, 'When you give a luncheon or a dinner, do not invite your friends or your brothers or your relatives or rich neighbours, in case they might invite you in return... But when you give a banquet, invite the poor, the crippled, the lame, and the blind. And you will be blessed, because they cannot repay you, for you will be repaid at the resurrection of the righteous.'

Neither Jesus nor Aidan allowed the rigid boundaries of their respective societies to prevent them from challenging the injustices they witnessed. As a guest at the house of a leading Pharisee, Jesus must surely have offended his host by failing to show him due deference. Jesus first addresses the assumption of precedence among the guests (vv. 7–11) and then turns his attention to his host (vv. 12–14), challenging him as to his motives in inviting those who have come. In both instances, Jesus is impelled by a vision of the kingdom, where all live with a spirit of inclusivity and generosity rather than narrow self-interest.

Like Jesus, Aidan also had no fear of challenging the rich: 'If wealthy people did wrong, he never kept silent out of respect or fear, but corrected them outspokenly' (*EH*, p. 150). He also challenged unjust social structures by using money given him by the rich 'to ransom any who had been unjustly sold as slaves' (*EH*, p. 150).

Reflection and prayer

'Have mercy on me, O God, according to your steadfast love; according to your abundant mercy blot out my transgressions... You desire truth in the inward being; therefore teach me wisdom in my secret heart'
(Psalm 51:1, 6).

BARBARA MOSSE

Colossians 3:12–15 (NRSV)

The values of the kingdom

As God's chosen ones, holy and beloved, clothe yourselves with compassion, kindness, humility, meekness, and patience. Bear with one another and, if anyone has a complaint against another, forgive each other; just as the Lord has forgiven you, so you also must forgive. Above all, clothe yourselves with love, which binds everything together in perfect harmony. And let the peace of Christ rule in your hearts, to which indeed you were called in the one body. And be thankful.

We shall return to Aidan for his special day at the end of next week, but, for now, we leave him with Bede's summary of his gifts and qualities: 'He cultivated peace and love, purity and humility; he was above anger and greed, and despised pride and conceit; he set himself to keep as well as to teach the laws of God, and was diligent in study and prayer. He used his priestly authority to check the proud and powerful; he tenderly comforted the sick; he relieved and protected the poor' (*EH*, p. 170).

One of the things that many modern readers find difficult when attempting to read the early saints' lives is the fact that they seem in some ways to be hardly human. They appear to have been paragons of perfection and workers of miracles. How can we take such writings seriously?

To conclude this is to miss the point. The authors of such lives were not setting out to paint a gritty, 'warts and all' portrait. Rather, the aim was to demonstrate the saint as a true reflection of Christ and, therefore, a key representative of his kingdom. Bede himself wrote two lives of Cuthbert and was very aware of the conventions of such writing. The verses from Colossians today are addressed to a holy people, consecrated to God's purposes, and Bede's summary of Aidan's qualities is a striking echo of them. In Bede's mind, Aidan was not simply bringing the gospel but he was also instigating a whole new community living and breathing the values of the kingdom.

Reflection

'Your kingdom come. Your will be done, on earth as it is in heaven'
(Matthew 6:10).

Barbara Mosse

Inspired by the saints

Therefore, since we are surrounded by so great a cloud of witnesses, let us also lay aside every weight and the sin that clings so closely, and let us run with perseverance the race that is set before us, looking to Jesus the pioneer and perfecter of our faith, who for the sake of the joy that was set before him endured the cross, disregarding its shame, and has taken his seat at the right hand of the throne of God.

Yesterday's passage painted a picture of the way of life the Christian community should pursue; today, the writer to the Hebrews exhorts the faith community to continue to endure persecution. They are not alone, but are surrounded by 'a great cloud of witnesses'—those who have preceded them in the life of faith and are now with God. As a young man, Cuthbert had a spiritual experience that may resonate with this. As he was praying and tending his flock in the hills one night, 'Cuthbert… suddenly saw light streaming from the skies, breaking the night's long darkness, and the choirs of the heavenly host coming down to earth. They quickly took into their ranks a human soul [Aidan], marvellously bright, and returned to their home above' (Bede, *Life of Cuthbert* [LC], pp. 47–48).

Cuthbert's vision of Aidan's soul being carried to heaven may be difficult to grasp, but to dismiss it on those grounds would be to miss the point. The vision convinced him that he should offer his whole life to God and he subsequently entered the monastery at Melrose. Bede's words need to be read against the backdrop of the scriptural 'cloud of witnesses': the light is passed on and Christians are part of an unending stream of witness stretching back to the beginning of time. Notice, too, the other scriptural resonances. Cuthbert, like David, was a young shepherd at the time of his call (1 Samuel 16:11–13) and the vision involving a heavenly host echoes the experience of the shepherds who were 'keeping watch' on the night of Christ's birth (Luke 2:8–15).

Reflection

Ponder today the teaching that we are each part of a living community of saints stretching through all time.

BARBARA MOSSE

JOHN 2:1–3, 7–11 (NRSV, ABRIDGED)

The pattern of Christ

On the third day there was a wedding in Cana of Galilee… When the wine gave out, the mother of Jesus said to him, 'They have no wine.'… Jesus said to [the servants], 'Fill the jars with water… Now draw some out, and take it to the chief steward.'… When the steward tasted the water that had become wine… [he] called the bridegroom and said to him, 'Everyone serves the good wine first, and then the inferior wine… But you have kept the good wine until now.' Jesus did this, the first of his signs, in Cana of Galilee, and revealed his glory; and his disciples believed in him.

In his *Life of Cuthbert*, Bede tells of an occasion when Cuthbert was offered hospitality by a convent of nuns who lived close to the mouth of the Tyne. After the meal, Cuthbert was asked whether he would like wine or beer to drink: '"Give me water," came the reply. It was drawn from the wells and brought. He blessed it, drank a little, and gave it to his priest, who gave it to… a priest of the monastery… The priest drank, and it seemed to him that the water had taken on the taste of wine' (*LC*, pp. 86–87).

Time and again in the lives of the saints, we find incidents that echo events in Christ's life. Despite years of critical and scholarly analysis, the account of the miracle at Cana remains, thankfully, an enigma. John describes it as the first of Jesus' signs (v. 11) and we need to allow its dissonance and its mystery to stand and continue to challenge us. Bede's intention is different. Here, we cannot know whether the water really had become wine or the priest who drank it was simply overwhelmed by the power of auto-suggestion in Cuthbert's presence, but that is not the point. The miracle's real meaning lies in the perceived Christlikeness of Cuthbert's life and its effect on those around him.

Reflection and prayer

'Put on the Lord Jesus Christ, and make no provision for the flesh'
(Romans 13:14). The early saints were depicted as 'patterns' of Christ.
How might the lives of contemporary saints appear to us today?

BARBARA MOSSE

Tuesday 27 August

MARK 6:7–9, 12–13, 30–31 (NRSV, ABRIDGED)

Balance of life

[Jesus] called the twelve and began to send them out two by two... He ordered them to take nothing for their journey except a staff; no bread, no bag, no money in their belts; but to wear sandals and not to put on two tunics... So they went out and proclaimed that all should repent. They cast out many demons, and anointed with oil many who were sick and cured them... [On their return] the apostles gathered around Jesus, and told him all that they had done and taught. He said to them, 'Come away to a deserted place all by yourselves and rest a while.' For many were coming and going, and they had no leisure even to eat.

The strains and stresses of an often frantically busy life are nothing new, as this incident from Mark's Gospel shows. The disciples return from their mission exhilarated but exhausted and Jesus immediately recognises their need to withdraw for a time, to rest and recuperate—and eat. The needs on this occasion were physical, but elsewhere in the Gospels Jesus makes it abundantly clear that there is also a need for spiritual withdrawal, however pressing and relentless are the demands from other people (Matthew 14:13; Luke 9:18; John 6:15).

Cuthbert experienced the same tension in his hugely busy ministry. On one occasion he was forcibly persuaded from his hermitage on the island of Inner Farne and compelled to be a bishop. He found this hugely distressing and his way of coping was to take with him the framework of prayer and worship developed in his monastic life. This then became the container and sustainer of all the activity he was called on to engage in: '[Cuthbert] strictly maintained his old frugality and took delight in preserving the rigours of the monastery amidst the pomp of the world. He fed the hungry, clothed the destitute, and had all the other marks of a perfect bishop' (LC, p. 77).

Reflection

Lay before God today your own life, with all its demands and obligations. Reflect on how you might create a framework that respects your need for both rest and recreation and time alone with God. Both Jesus and Cuthbert needed this and you are no different!

BARBARA MOSSE

For God alone

> For God alone my soul waits in silence; from him comes my salva-
> tion. He alone is my rock and my salvation, my fortress; I shall never
> be shaken. How long will you assail a person, will you batter your
> victim, all of you, as you would a leaning wall, a tottering fence? ...
> For God alone my soul waits in silence, for my hope is from him.

In a psalm traditionally attributed to David, the psalmist's voice echoes
across the centuries, affirming his faith and trust that God will save and
preserve him in the midst of suffering and the attacks of his enemies.
David's vocation from God was to assume the kingship of Israel after
the failure of Saul—a life of intense activity and public responsibility.
These words, though, uttered during the crisis of an enemy attack, hint
at another kind of vocation.

Cuthbert was able to live out this other kind of vocation—in part.
Interspersed between periods of intense activity, he also experienced
a call to the contemplative solitude of hermit life, lived out initially on
St Cuthbert's Isle (just off Lindisfarne). Latterly, when the need for
greater solitude grew pressing, he lived completely alone on the island
of Inner Farne, spending his time in prayer.

In today's overactive church, the vocation to contemplative prayer
often tends to be seen as some kind of escape or abdication of responsibility. It may be just about tolerated when a person is sick, elderly
or housebound, when the perception may be that they are no longer
able to do anything more 'useful', but any thought that a younger
person may receive such a call to prayer as their primary 'work' is met
with incredulity. Yet God does continue to call people to this work, as
the growing numbers of hermits—of all ages and from all walks of
life—bears witness. Their dedication is a sign for us all, pointing to
Christians' fundamental responsibility to grow and deepen in their
relationship with God.

Reflection

*'For God alone my soul waits in silence' (Psalm 62:1). How receptive are
we to the call to prayer as a primary vocation, whether in our own lives or
the lives of others?*

BARBARA MOSSE

A holy death

David said: 'Blessed are you, O Lord, the God of our ancestor Israel, for ever and ever... But who am I, and what is my people, that we should be able to make this freewill offering?... I know, my God, that you search the heart, and take pleasure in upright-ness; in the uprightness of my heart I have freely offered all these things, and now I have seen your people... offering freely and joyously to you. O Lord... keep for ever such purposes and thoughts in the hearts of your people, and direct their hearts towards you. Grant to my son Solomon that with single mind he may keep your commandments... and that he may build the tem-ple for which I have made provision.'

The final words of the dying have always been eagerly garnered, treas-ured and remembered, the hope being that, in this summation of a life, will be distilled the wisdom of the years. In 1 Chronicles' recording of David's final prayer, the tone is joyous and exuberant and David func-tions as the voice of the worshipping community as he returns praise to God for all the blessings on his life. A word of caution is in order here, however, as the words recorded may also bear something of the scribe's agenda (compare them with David's 'last words' as found in 1 Kings 2:1–9!)

Cuthbert's words were also of enormous importance to his followers, although the influence of the scribe was also detectable in them as Cuthbert's authority was used to stress and enforce Roman practices. Nonetheless, the plea to 'preserve amongst yourselves unfailing divine charity... live in mutual accord with all other servants of Christ' (*LC*, p. 93) certainly carries the authentic ring of the saint.

Despite any political or personal bias, something vital still remains. As death approaches, there is a need to put one's house in order, to look back with gratitude and contrition and lay down willingly the gift of our lives so that we may return to God. How prepared are we for this?

Reflection

Teach me to live, that I may dread the grave as little as my bed.

Thomas Ken, 1695

Barbara Mosse

Martyrs for Christ

Others were tortured, refusing to accept release, in order to obtain a better resurrection. Others suffered mocking and flogging, and even chains and imprisonment. They were stoned to death, they were sawn in two, they were killed by the sword; they went about in skins of sheep and goats, destitute, persecuted, tormented—of whom the world was not worthy. They wandered in deserts and mountains, and in caves and holes in the ground.

In the Anglo-Saxon Chronicle for the year 793, we read, 'In this year terrible portents appeared over Northumbria, and miserably afflicted the inhabitants: these were exceptional flashes of lightning, and fiery dragons were seen flying in the air, and soon followed a great famine, and after that in the same year the harrying of the heathen miserably destroyed God's church in Lindisfarne by rapine and slaughter' (pp. 54, 56).

The persecution of Christians was nothing new, as the graphic description in today's passage makes clear. Even so, the shocking Viking attack on the Lindisfarne monastery stunned the community and marked the beginning of the end of its place as the centre of ministry and mission in Northumbria. Those who survived the initial onslaught stayed on the island a while longer, but, as Viking attacks intensified, life became increasingly difficult. Cuthbert had died in 687 and, finally, his community was forced to leave, taking Cuthbert's body with them as they moved inland to safer sites, eventually settling at Durham.

Although separated by many centuries, the events described in both Hebrews and the Anglo-Saxon Chronicle developed along similar lines. The Christian community, harassed by non-believers, is compelled to scatter. The early Christians 'wandered in deserts and mountains'; the Lindisfarne monks became a community on the move. In more recent times, the persecuted church in repressive states has endured a similar pattern, being been forced to go 'underground'. How well would our own faith stand up to such pressure? Would we be prepared to die for it?

Reflection

'This child is destined… to be a sign that will be opposed… and a sword will pierce your own soul too' (Luke 2:34–35).

BARBARA MOSSE

Aidan: apostle to the English

Am I not free? Am I not an apostle? Have I not seen Jesus our Lord? Are you not my work in the Lord? If I am not an apostle to others, at least I am to you; for you are the seal of my apostleship in the Lord.

Today we celebrate the feast of Aidan and our 'Lindisfarne cycle' comes full circle. The debt we owe him is immense. The 19th-century Bishop Lightfoot of Durham once wanted to express just how significant an impact he felt Aidan had had, not only on Northumbria but also all the other parts of the country that were subsequently evangelised by the monks from Lindisfarne. Lightfoot memorably stated, 'Augustine was the Apostle of Kent, but Aidan was the Apostle of England.'

What is it that makes an apostle—what are the essential characteristics? Paul certainly had to fight his corner on this one, as his claim to apostleship was initially treated with suspicion by the Jerusalem apostles. This was partly on account of his past as a dogged and determined persecutor of Christians (Acts 9:26) and partly also because the idea of Paul as an apostle to the Gentiles only grew over time (Galatians 1 and 2). The term *apostolos* in the original Greek means 'messenger' or 'one who is sent'—a function clearly fulfilled by both Paul and Aidan. As to what the ideal qualities are of such a person, we return to Bede's account of Aidan, which offers words that could equally be used to describe both: 'He cultivated peace and love, purity and humility; he was above anger and greed, and despised pride and conceit; he set himself to keep as well as teach the laws of God... he... laboured diligently to cultivate the faith, piety and love that marks out God's saints' (EH, pp. 170, 186).

Reflection

'Go therefore and make disciples of all nations, baptising them in the name of the Father and of the Son and of the Holy Spirit, and teaching them to obey everything that I have commanded you. And remember, I am with you always, to the end of the age' (Matthew 28:19–20).

Barbara Mosse

The BRF
Magazine

The Managing Editor writes…   140

International Messy Church   141
Lucy Moore

New editor for *Quiet Spaces*   144
Sally Smith

Recommended reading   146

Extract from *Spiritual Care of Dying and Bereaved People* 149
Penelope Wilcock

Order Forms

Supporting BRF's Ministry   151
BRF Ministry Appeal Response Form   153
BRF Publications   155
Subscriptions   156

The Managing Editor writes...

Spirituality, discipleship and mission—we sometimes talk about these elements of Christian life as if they're separate from each other, almost in different 'boxes'. Perhaps we think of spirituality as for the more contemplative among us, discipleship for the practical servant types and mission for the self-confident extraverts. Yet all three are interrelated and are all important parts of BRF's overall vision.

In her report on 'International Messy Church', Lucy Moore expresses a sense of great excitement as Messy Church continues to spread worldwide, with ever-expanding networks of people involved in this mission to families outside 'traditional' church. Our 'Recommended reading' in this issue also offers books that focus on the more outward-looking elements—evangelism in today's culture, discipleship in Messy Church and active service in the church and the world.

In the third of these books, *Servant Ministry*, Tony Horsfall writes, 'The reflective life... is valid only if it is expressed outwardly in tangible acts of service, and love for God is real only when it leads to love for others.' But of course (as I'm sure Tony would agree), when we love and serve others, and when we engage with people outside the church, we become more and more aware of the needs in the world around us, which sends us back to reflection and prayer—and so the cycle goes on.

Sally Smith's article on our revamped creative prayer and spirituality journal, *Quiet Spaces*, describes a new direction for the journal, which we hope will stimulate readers (as Sally says) 'to grow in their relationship with God and to keep prayer as a central part of their lives'. Finally, our chosen book extract, from *Spiritual Care of Dying and Bereaved People*, focuses on the spiritual identity at the the core of every individual.

Whatever we consider to be our own major gifts and calling in the Christian life, spirituality, discipleship and mission are all equally vital, each interwoven with and constantly feeding into one another. We hope that BRF can continue to inspire you to develop all three strands in your own walk with God.

Lisa Cherrett

International
Messy Church

Lucy Moore

'All the ends of the earth will remember and
turn to the Lord, and all the families of the
nations will bow down before him' (Psalm
22:27, NIV). When he mentions 'bowing', I don't think the psalmist had in mind painting, constructing, exploding, glueing, jumping,
inventing, dancing, running, shouting, laughing and eating before the
Lord, but perhaps he would have been happy to know that so many
families from so many nations across the world take such delight in
their Lord and Creator, albeit expressing it in different ways.

We've been thrilled and intrigued to see Messy Church spreading to
different countries and continents over the last eight years, and to hear
stories of families all over the world coming back to church, or coming
to church for the first time, and enjoying it enough to keep coming.

Back in the ancient history of seven years ago, when Messy Church
was just a handful of local churches giving it a try, Fresh Expressions
came across the idea and asked if they could film it for their first DVD
promoting the idea of fresh expressions of church. The DVD was duly
despatched to Fresh Expressions associates, who used it in their training across the world. Very early in the development of Messy Church,
therefore, we were receiving emails from countries as far flung as New
Zealand and Canada, asking how they could get going with a Messy
Church of their own. 'We saw it in the DVD and it looks really good…'

There is also a certain amount of gossip! People from our own
church came back from a cruise describing how they had befriended
an Australian couple, had found out they were all Christians and had
started sharing stories of what their different churches do, including
Messy Church. 'And they were so interested! They want to start one in
Adelaide! Now I must send them a book about it!'

We currently have several international speakers who are enthusi-
astic to include Messy Church as a tool for churches to use. Our dear
Danish friend, Bjarne Gertz Olsen, speaks at many events in Eastern
Europe and emailed today saying, 'Soon I shall go to Slovakia to

European Lutheran Sunday School Associations conference. Here will be participants from… Germany, Georgia, Belarus, Ukraine, Poland, Slovakia, Estonia, Latvia, Romania, Denmark. I will like here to make an exhibition about Messy Church and also inform about Messy Church.'

As you can imagine, the impact of sharing the idea across all those countries could be huge. Another friend, Marty Woods from Fusion, has been speaking around the world at different training events and emailed, 'We have just come back from a Sports Conference in Orlando… Great time: 127 countries with over 540 people… Many are interested in Messy Church—particularly in the Ukraine. They have 15,000 churches that they are contacting and working with in some way, preparing for the Euro Cup. They respond most to the idea of the Sunday after the Opening Ceremony having a Messy Church…' and later: 'Been on the move, flying back from Poland, and they are really keen about Messy Church there. Plan to run them after our festivals at the Euro Cup in at least three places I am aware of.'

So where do we know of Messy Churches happening outside the UK? The countries we *know* of are Canada, New Zealand, Australia, the USA, Denmark, Germany, Poland, South Africa, Switzerland, Norway, Grenada, Spain, Ireland and the Falklands. Some of these have just one isolated Messy Church: Spain's was set up in the English Chaplaincy on the Costa del Sol after I spoke at the Synod in Portugal. South Africa's is run by someone who came across the idea while visiting relatives in the UK. Poland's was started by a Salvation Army officer who had been introduced to the idea through her Army networks. Switzerland's is, again, a set of family relationships sharing a good thing around. The way Kreativ Kirke began in Norway remains a mystery!

Sue Kalbfleisch and Nancy Rowe are doing a fantastic job in Eastern Canada, leading training and keeping Messy Churches in touch with each other, and there are at least 20 happening there. One vicar has written her academic research on it. There isn't much encouragement from the church authorities there yet, but we hope and trust that there will be when they understand more about it.

In New Zealand, Julie Hintz is building a network and series of training events for their growing numbers of Messy Churches. They prefer to be reasonably independent of 'colonial' ideas so we are encouraging a sense of interdependence and working with Julie to create good links.

Australia feels full of Messy friends since our trips in 2011 and 2012, and Sydney-based Judyth Roberts is responding to requests for help there as part of her job within the Uniting Church.

In the States, we are looking forward to things taking off after my trip to the USA in November, which may focus the energy building up there through isolated Messy Churches and through the efforts of Andrew Holmes, Our Man in Indianapolis.

Denmark is an interesting case as they have worked from top down rather than grassroots up like the rest of us. The Danish Sunday School Association became excited about the book and concept when talking to Richard and Karen at the Frankfurt Book Fair and decided to go for it wholeheartedly as an organisation, with their own website and resources in Danish. They currently have about 25 Messy Churches, backed by a Regional Coordinator, Karen Markusson.

Charis Lambert took Messy Church out to Zimbabwe with members of her team and the Zimkids charity. She writes of one of the events they led:

Our Messy Church in Mutoko started a day earlier than expected as 60 people turned up at the church, having walked 14km to see us. We could not disappoint their enthusiasm so we spent a couple of hours with them making bracelets, playing with playdough and introducing them to our parachute games, before giving them some sandwiches and sending them home. To our amazement they all returned the next morning for more! …

Our training was simplified for this very mixed-age audience and needed to be translated into Shona by the local pastor and our Zimkids team… We sat everyone under the trees and realised that we had about 200 people sitting together. We demonstrated how to fold paper and make a cross with just one cut—to show how useful it is to do something in order to aid our understanding. We started some singing and were blown away by the exuberance of the Shona worship! After lunch, people kept on arriving, adding themselves to the already overcrowded parachutes, the games of soccer and the craft activities—more donkeys!

We finished the afternoon at about 5pm after serving tea to approximately 300 people—no mean feat in a church with no kitchen facilities and no electricity or running water!

At BRF we have the interesting job of trying to balancing the needs of the UK Messy network with the needs of the networks in other countries, trying to respond appropriately and effectively without killing off the team members with excessive travel demands. But most of all we have the privilege of getting excited by and with this wonderful movement of God's Spirit as he finds his way to reach families in so many different places and contexts.

Lucy Moore heads up BRF's Messy Church ministry. For more information, visit www.messychurch.org.uk.

New editor for *Quiet Spaces*

Sally Smith

Until recently I worked in education publishing, producing materials for teaching Christianity in RE lessons. My work there built on years spent in classrooms and gave me a new set of skills in editing and project management. But then I heard I was being made redundant. After the normal panic, I began to wonder what I could do. The whole process was steeped in prayer, with many people praying for and with me, and, in a strange way, I felt privileged to recognise God's involvement in the whole process. God didn't tell me what was next; he just promised that the future would contain gold and jewels.

I like to have everything planned out so, although this was comforting, it was also, to my eyes, unsatisfactory: what would a 'gold' future look like? What would I be doing? What reason would I have to get up in the morning? How was God going to weave together the editing, spirituality and education strands that were all equally important to me? But God was true to his promise and provided more than I could have imagined.

I had long used and admired *Quiet Spaces* so being asked to take the best of *Quiet Spaces* and merge it with the concept of Bible reading notes seemed a dream request. I was being asked to produce the publication I had been looking for on bookshop shelves but had failed to find. At first it felt self-indulgent: imagine what you would like and then make it happen! But as I talked to other people about the idea, I was encouraged: they were asking when it would be out and how they could get a copy. They wanted to develop their prayer life and keep it fresh and creative. Bible reading notes provided a brilliant structure and were feeding these people intellectually, but they were looking for something else as well, for ways of engaging with God on a different level. They wanted to develop their walk with God in practical ways.

So the idea grew. Take a theme for two weeks and explore that theme in a range of different ways, allowing for different personalities and styles. Include some classic writers on prayer, some traditional approaches, and be creative and innovative as well.

It soon became apparent that the format needed to be flexible. It would be no good telling readers to explore a Bible passage artistically on a day when they barely had time to stop—if on another day they could devote a whole hour or so to a prayer walk. So the individual elements needed to be undated, with readers being encouraged to use the most appropriate element for them on any particular day. The message would be: if you miss a day or find something that doesn't appeal, that's OK, you can try something else. If you only get halfway through, you can come back and finish it tomorrow. Or you can do several elements in one day, creating a personal quiet day when you have time and space to try something new.

There began to be a rhythm to each theme, with some elements being longer or shorter, more or less involved, active, creative or thoughtful. The rhythm fitted across a day—from the morning, when concentration levels are often higher, through to the afternoon, when concentration is lower and something more active or practical is useful, and on into the evening, when we often become more reflective and want to look back on the day. The rhythm worked across a week as well, with some days when we have energy and time and are able to put more of ourselves into our prayer life, and other days when we just want to be fed.

With this flexibility came a sense of freedom. Readers could use the material as suited them best, but there was always the possibility of simply taking one element a day and working through the book in order. There are times when we need the comfort that such structures bring.

I have tried to include some of the classic writers on prayer, to explore how we can learn from them, as well as using the Bible in prayer and, of course, retaining the themes that *Quiet Spaces* has traditionally been so good at addressing. The writers have come up with some creative ways of entering the themes and responding to them, enabling readers to grow in their relationship with God and to keep prayer as a central part of their lives.

It has certainly been a period of gold and jewels for me, bringing together my editing skills and my experience of leading and attending quiet days and retreats. It has been an exciting adventure to produce the new *Quiet Spaces*. I have worked with some great writers who have caught the vision and produced excellent materials, which have already enhanced my prayer life, leading me on that journey to and with God.

Sally Smith is a spiritual director in Southwell and Nottingham diocese, where she also leads quiet days and is part of a deanery group exploring spirituality outside the church. She has a Diploma in Theological and Pastoral Studies.

Recommended reading

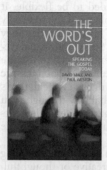

Our recommended reading for this issue focuses on the important question of church and how it can bring its mission strategy and tactics up to date, to address today's challenges. How can the issues of effectively engaging unchurched local communities be explained and taken forward? How does the church move people within its influence to a deeper commitment—beyond theoretical faith to real discipleship? What are the responsibilities of those who support leaders in their task of contemporary evangelism and discipleship? These are not new questions, but declining church attendance demands a revaluation of the current approach. BRF is pleased to offer this group of new titles to further the progress of the debate and help provide solutions to these vital issues.

The Word's Out
Speaking the gospel today
David Male and Paul Weston

At a time when few people attend church, evangelism is more important than ever. The problem is that churches and individuals often struggle with the idea because their approach is no longer culturally appropriate.

This book aims to reform, reimagine and renew a theology, vision and practice for evangelism. An invaluable resource for church leaders, its approach is theologically rigorous and powerfully practical, focusing on redefining a genuine biblical evangelism. What does it mean to be an 'evangelist' now? If it isn't our primary gifting, how can we facilitate it in our church? And how can we connect not just with those on the fringes but with those who are way outside?

The Revd David Male is Director of the Centre for Pioneer Learning and Tutor in Pioneer Mission Training at Ridley Hall and Westcott House, Cambridge, and Fresh Expressions Adviser for Ely Diocese. The Revd Dr Paul Weston is Tutor in Mission and Homiletics at Ridley Hall, Cambridge.

paperback, 978 0 85746 169 8, £8.99, 224 pages
Also available for Kindle: please visit www.brfonline.org.uk/ebooks/

Making Disciples in Messy Church
Growing faith in an all-age community
Paul Moore

'Messy Church needs to reinvent discipleship!' These words from Paul Butler, Bishop of Southwell and Nottingham, in April 2011, may seem alarming at first. Why does a new form of church that has proved highly successful in attracting unchurched families need to reinvent Christian discipleship? What's wrong with current church methods?

The fact is, as Paul Moore (husband of Messy Church founder Lucy Moore) points out, that current approaches are failing, leaving faith largely theoretical and private, and giving little hope of personal motivation. This is not the way forward to more vibrant church communities.

Moore's assessment is that many assumptions need examining about how people come to faith and about what we understand by discipleship. For all churches it is necessary to ask what is happening in the lives of people coming to church. What wisdom can be found in scripture, Christian tradition and human experience that can help us present the gospel in a way that encourages response?

So what does Moore think his Messy Churchgoers need, to move them forward from Messy Church attendance to an active faith?

First we need to facilitate more openness through positive experiences of Christian community and building relationships and trust. Then there are subsequent stages in which we gradually introduce people to Jesus and the gospel, help them to take their first steps of faith and provide the right learning environment for lifelong growth in discipleship.

These are the issues that Paul engages with in this insightful new book. It's essential reading for Messy Church teams but will also be beneficial for any church battling with the issues of evangelism and discipleship in a contemporary context.

paperback, 978 0 85746 218 3, £6.99, 128 pages
Also available for Kindle: please visit www.brfonline.org.uk/ebooks/

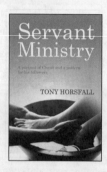

Servant Ministry
A portrait of Christ and a pattern for his followers
Tony Horsfall

The words 'servant ministry' may immediately suggest to you that this is a book just for church leaders, but stop right there. What if the term should be rightly applied to all Christians?

Tony Horsfall is convinced that an understanding of servanthood is vital for the health of local churches in this period of 'exile'—church on the fringe of society. Every member needs to appreciate their role as a servant of God, because ordinary lives that demonstrate a Christian commitment are a starting-point for engaging non-churchgoers.

In *Servant Ministry*, Tony offers a practical exposition of the first 'Servant Song' in Isaiah (42:1–9). He applies insights drawn from the passage to topics such as the motivation for service and the call to serve; valid expressions of servanthood and the link between evangelism and social action; character formation and what it means to be a servant; how to keep going over the long haul and the importance of listening to God on a daily basis, over a lifetime.

paperback, 978 085746 088 2, £7.99, 144 pages
Also available for Kindle: please visit www.brfonline.org.uk/ebooks/

To order copies of any of these books, please turn to the order form on page 155, or visit www.brfonline.org.uk.

An extract from
Spiritual Care of Dying and Bereaved People

Spiritual Care of Dying and Bereaved People is a fresh, original and honest look at death and bereavement, including the author's personal experiences. Penelope Wilcock encourages readers to grow in confidence as companions, facing the questions people ask and offering a reflection on the kind of God those questions reveal. The following extract is taken from Part One of the book.

This book is about life, not death. Spending time with hospice patients in the 1980s and early '90s, the atmosphere of expectancy often struck me. When we are with people approaching death, we feel a sense of awe, the solemnity of a great moment approaching—a sacred moment…

Finding and accepting identity

Before anything else, spiritual care is about identity. Prayer, religion, philosophy, sacraments—all may play their part but, first and foremost, spiritual care is about identity.

Spirituality is all about who one is, and that is found only in relationship: with other people, the ones who make up our world, and with the foundational reality that believers call God.

For proper spiritual care to be given, there must be an affirmation of the dying or bereaved person's identity as a unique individual… as a spiritual free self, a being of dignity and worth. It is important that those who select and appoint spiritual carers look for people who regard others in that way, who will hear and see and never patronise. I am not sure that this quality in a spiritual carer can be taught: perhaps it is an awakening, a realisation, able to be recognised but not communicated… Techniques of care and listening can be taught, but not that fundamental vision of the spirituality of human encounter.

Terminal illness mounts a serious attack on the sense of identity. The powerlessness, loneliness and fear commonly experienced feel dehumanising and alienating, and constitute (or trigger) spiritual crisis in many people…

It is virtually impossible to maintain spiritual equilibrium when one's own entire being is coming apart; when physical functioning is haywire, mental processes are embarrassingly unpredictable, and emotions are ricocheting all over the place in the desperate attempt to adjust, to assimilate and to maintain the dignity of appearing normal.

The sense of self is enhanced by creating an environment for the self to live in. My choice of clothes, whether I live in a flat or a house, the fabrics and carpeting and furniture I have chosen, my ornaments and pictures and crockery, whether I eat supper at the table or curled up on the sofa with a tray on my lap, whether I decorate my home with tree and lights and tinsel at Christmas or put candles on the table for a dinner party, if I keep a cat as a companion—all of this is how I offer my identity to the world and arrive at a sense of self…

People in terminal illness often have to face the decision to sell their home. They have to find a new home for beloved pet animals that must be left behind now. In hospital they may be encouraged to wear night-clothes. The choice of how or when or what to eat is limited by the possibilities of institutional provision. No more candles on the dinner table; no longer my plates, my wallpaper, my sofa. People who appreci-ate enormously the care and love they are given still sit in the beds of caring institutions, saying with tears in their eyes, 'It's so hard to give up my home.' …

Good spiritual care understands that it is not things that have been lost to a terminally ill person coming into institutional care; it is the self. Like a dance or a song or a painting, the environment of home was the person's song of creation in the world: to lose it is to lose one's own space, to live in the world as a refugee…

Spiritual care involves nurturing again the bruised and diminished sense of self. This happens through the stimulus of relationship and interaction as carers bring their individual personalities to the situation, being self-expressive and self-giving without being self-indulgent…

The person's individuality and identity should be affirmed by the spiritual carer in creating a sense of not rushing, and a sense of private space in loving and respectful body language, maybe using touch. Any religious or ideological concerns of the patient should be recognised and maybe mentioned. Above all else, till the last breath, this is a person with a name, a shining light of selfhood, dust of Adam, of Eve, brought into life by the breath of the living God.

To order a copy of this book, please turn to the order form on page 155, or visit www.brfonline.org.uk.

SUPPORTING BRF'S MINISTRY

As a Christian charity, BRF is involved in seven distinct yet complementary areas.

- **BRF** (www.brf.org.uk) resources adults for their spiritual journey through Bible reading notes, books and Quiet Days. BRF also provides the infrastructure that supports our other specialist ministries.
- **Foundations21** (www.foundations21.net) provides flexible and innovative ways for individuals and groups to explore their Christian faith and discipleship through a multimedia internet-based resource.
- **Messy Church** (www.messychurch.org.uk), led by Lucy Moore, enables churches all over the UK (and increasingly abroad) to reach children and adults beyond the fringes of the church.
- **Barnabas in Churches** (www.barnabasinchurches.org.uk) helps churches to support, resource and develop their children's ministry with the under-11s more effectively .
- **Barnabas in Schools** (www.barnabasinschools.org.uk) enables primary school children and teachers to explore Christianity creatively and bring the Bible alive within RE and Collective Worship.
- **Faith in Homes** (www.faithinhomes.org.uk) supports families to explore and live out the Christian faith at home.
- **Who Let The Dads Out** (www.wholetthedadsout.org) inspires churches to engage with dads and their pre-school children.

At the heart of BRF's ministry is a desire to equip adults and children for Christian living—helping them to read and understand the Bible, explore prayer and grow as disciples of Jesus. We need your help to make an impact on the local church, local schools and the wider community.

- You could support BRF's ministry with a donation or standing order (using the response form overleaf).
- You could consider making a bequest to BRF in your will.
- You could encourage your church to support BRF as part of your church's giving to home mission—perhaps focusing on a specific area of our ministry, or a particular member of our Barnabas team.
- Most important of all, you could support BRF with your prayers.

If you would like to discuss how a specific gift or bequest could be used in the development of our ministry, please phone 01865 319700 or email enquiries@brf.org.uk.

Whatever you can do or give, we thank you for your support.

Thank you for reading BRF Bible reading notes. BRF has been producing a variety of Bible reading notes for over 90 years, helping people all over the UK and the world connect with the Bible on a personal level every day.

Could you help us find other people who would enjoy our notes?

We produce a Bible Reading Resource Pack for church groups to use to encourage regular Bible reading.

This FREE pack contains:

- Samples of all BRF Bible reading notes.
- Our Resources for Personal Bible Reading catalogue, providing all you need to know about our Bible reading notes.
- A ready-to-use church magazine feature about BRF notes.
- Ready-made sermon and all-age service ideas to help your church into the Bible (ideal for Bible Sunday events).
- And much more!

How to order your FREE pack:

- Visit: www.biblereadingnotes.org.uk/request-a-bible-reading-resources-pack/
- Telephone: 01865 319700 between 9.15 and 17.30
- Post: Complete the form below and post to: Bible Reading Resource Pack, BRF, 15 The Chambers, Vineyard, Abingdon, OX14 3FE

Name _____

Address _____

_____ Postcode _____

Telephone _____

Email _____

Please send me _____ Bible Reading Resources Pack(s)

This pack is produced free of charge for all UK addresses but, if you wish to offer a donation towards our costs, this would be appreciated. If you require a pack to be sent outside of the UK, please contact us for details of postage and packing charges. Tel: +44 1865 319700. Thank you.

BRF MINISTRY APPEAL RESPONSE FORM

Name _____

Address _____

_____ Postcode _____

Telephone _____ Email _____

Standing Order – Banker's Order

❏ I would like to support BRF's ministry with a regular donation by standing order

To the Manager, Name of Bank/Building Society

Address _____

_____ Postcode _____

Sort Code _____ Account Name _____

Account No _____

Please pay Royal Bank of Scotland plc, Drummonds, 49 Charing Cross,
London SW1A 2DX (Sort Code 16-00-38), for the account of BRF A/C No. 00774151

The sum of _____ pounds on ___/___/___ (insert date) and thereafter the same amount
on the same day each month / same day annually (delete as applic.) until further notice.

Signature _____ Date _____

Single donation

❏ I enclose my cheque/credit card/Switch card details for a donation of
£5 £10 £25 £50 £100 £250 (other) £ _____ to support BRF's ministry.

Card no. [ ]

Expires [ ][ ][ ][ ]   Security code [ ][ ][ ]   Issue no. [ ][ ][ ][ ]

Signature _____ Date _____

Please use my donation for ❏ BRF   ❏ Foundations21   ❏ Messy Church
❏ Barnabas Children's Ministry   ❏ Faith in Homes

❏ Please send me information about making a bequest to BRF in my will.

If you would like to Gift Aid your donation, please fill in the form overleaf.

Please detach and send this completed form to: Richard Fisher, BRF,
15 The Chambers, Vineyard, Abingdon OX14 3FE. BRF is a Registered Charity (No.233280)

GIFT AID DECLARATION

Bible Reading Fellowship

Please treat as Gift Aid donations all qualifying gifts of money made
today ☐   in the past 4 years ☐   in the future ☐   (tick all that apply)

I confirm I have paid or will pay an amount of Income Tax and/or Capital Gains Tax for
each tax year (6 April to 5 April) that is at least equal to the amount of tax that all the
charities that I donate to will reclaim on my gifts for that tax year. I understand that other
taxes such as VAT or Council Tax do not qualify. I understand the charity will reclaim 28p
of tax on every £1 that I gave up to 5 April 2008 and will reclaim 25p of tax on every £1
that I give on or after 6 April 2008.

Donor's details

Title _____ First name or initials _____ Surname _____

Full home address _____

_____

Postcode _____

Date _____

Signature _____

Please notify Bible Reading Fellowship if you:
- want to cancel this declaration
- change your name or home address
- no longer pay sufficient tax on your income and/or capital gains.

If you pay Income Tax at the higher or additional rate and want to receive the
additional tax relief due to you, you must include all your Gift Aid donations on your
Self-Assessment tax return or ask HM Revenue and Customs to adjust your tax code.

ND0213

BRF PUBLICATIONS ORDER FORM

Please send me the following book(s):

		Quantity	Price	Total
169 8	The Word's Out (D. Male & P. Weston)	_____	£8.99	_____
218 3	Making Disciples in Messy Church (P. Moore)	_____	£6.99	_____
088 2	Servant Ministry (T. Horsfall)	_____	£7.99	_____
115 5	Spiritual Care Dying/Bereaved People (P. Wilcock)	_____	£9.99	_____
061 5	Family Fun for Summer (J. Butcher)	_____	£4.99	_____
139 1	Ten-Minute Summer Activity Book (B. James)	_____	£3.99	_____

Total cost of books £ _____
Donation £ _____
Postage and packing £ _____
TOTAL £ _____

POSTAGE AND PACKING CHARGES

order value	UK	Europe	Surface	Air Mail
£7.00 & under	£1.25	£3.00	£3.50	£5.50
£7.01–£30.00	£2.25	£5.50	£6.50	£10.00
Over £30.00	free	prices on request		

Please complete the payment details below and send with payment to: **BRF, 15 The Chambers, Vineyard, Abingdon OX14 3FE**

Name _____

Address _____

_____ Postcode _____

Tel _____ Email _____

Total enclosed £ _____ (cheques should be made payable to 'BRF')

Please charge my Visa ❑ Mastercard ❑ Switch card ❑ with £ _____

Card no: ☐☐☐☐ ☐☐☐☐ ☐☐☐☐ ☐☐☐☐ ☐☐☐☐

Expires ☐☐☐☐ Security code ☐☐☐

Issue no (Switch only) ☐☐☐☐

Signature (essential if paying by credit/Switch) _____

NEW DAYLIGHT INDIVIDUAL SUBSCRIPTIONS

❏ I would like to take out a subscription myself:

Your name _____

Your address _____

_____

_____ Postcode _____

Tel _____ Email _____

Please send *New Daylight* beginning with the September 2013 / January 2014 / May 2014 issue: (delete as applicable)

(please tick box)	UK	SURFACE	AIR MAIL
NEW DAYLIGHT	❏ £15.00	❏ £21.60	❏ £24.00
NEW DAYLIGHT 3-year sub	❏ £37.80		
NEW DAYLIGHT DELUXE	❏ £18.99	❏ £29.10	❏ £31.50
NEW DAYLIGHT daily email only	❏ £12.00 (UK and overseas)		

Please complete the payment details below and send with appropriate payment to: **BRF, 15 The Chambers, Vineyard, Abingdon OX14 3FE**

Total enclosed £ _____ (cheques should be made payable to 'BRF')

Please charge my Visa ❏ Mastercard ❏ Switch card ❏ with £ _____

Card no: ☐☐☐☐☐☐☐☐☐☐☐☐☐☐☐☐☐☐☐

Expires ☐☐☐☐ Security code ☐☐☐

Issue no (Switch only) ☐☐☐☐

Signature (essential if paying by card) _____

To set up a direct debit, please also complete the form on page 159 and send it to BRF with this form.

BRF is a Registered Charity

ND0213

NEW DAYLIGHT GIFT SUBSCRIPTIONS

❏ I would like to give a gift subscription (please provide both names and addresses:

Your name _____

Your address _____

_____ Postcode _____

Tel _____ Email _____

Gift subscription name _____

Gift subscription address _____

_____ Postcode _____

Gift message (20 words max. or include your own gift card for the recipient)

_____

_____

Please send *New Daylight* beginning with the September 2013 / January 2014 / May 2014 issue: (delete as applicable)

(please tick box)	UK	SURFACE	AIR MAIL
NEW DAYLIGHT	❏ £15.00	❏ £21.60	❏ £24.00
NEW DAYLIGHT 3-year sub	❏ £37.80		
NEW DAYLIGHT DELUXE	❏ £18.99	❏ £29.10	❏ £31.50
NEW DAYLIGHT daily email only	❏ £12.00 (UK and overseas)		

Please complete the payment details below and send with appropriate payment to: **BRF, 15 The Chambers, Vineyard, Abingdon OX14 3FE**

Total enclosed £ _____ (cheques should be made payable to 'BRF')

Please charge my Visa ❏ Mastercard ❏ Switch card ❏ with £ _____

Card no: ⬜⬜⬜⬜ ⬜⬜⬜⬜ ⬜⬜⬜⬜ ⬜⬜⬜⬜ ⬜⬜⬜⬜

Expires ⬜⬜⬜⬜ Security code ⬜⬜⬜

Issue no (Switch only) ⬜⬜⬜⬜

Signature (essential if paying by card) _____

To set up a direct debit, please also complete the form on page 159 and send it to BRF with this form.

DIRECT DEBIT PAYMENTS

Now you can pay for your annual subscription to BRF notes using Direct Debit. You need only give your bank details once, and the payment is made automatically every year until you cancel it. If you would like to pay by Direct Debit, please use the form opposite, entering your BRF account number under 'Reference'.

You are fully covered by the Direct Debit Guarantee:

The Direct Debit Guarantee

- This Guarantee is offered by all banks and building societies that accept instructions to pay Direct Debits.
- If there are any changes to the amount, date or frequency of your Direct Debit, The Bible Reading Fellowship will notify you 10 working days in advance of your account being debited or as otherwise agreed. If you request The Bible Reading Fellowship to collect a payment, confirmation of the amount and date will be given to you at the time of the request.
- If an error is made in the payment of your Direct Debit, by The Bible Reading Fellowship or your bank or building society, you are entitled to a full and immediate refund of the amount paid from your bank or building society.
  - If you receive a refund you are not entitled to, you must pay it back when The Bible Reading Fellowship asks you to.
- You can cancel a Direct Debit at any time by simply contacting your bank or building society. Written confirmation may be required. Please also notify us.

The Bible Reading Fellowship

Instruction to your bank or building society to pay by Direct Debit

Please fill in the whole form using a ballpoint pen and send to The Bible Reading Fellowship, 15 The Chambers, Vineyard, Abingdon OX14 3FE.

Service User Number: | 5 | 5 | 8 | 2 | 2 | 9 |

Name and full postal address of your bank or building society

To: The Manager	Bank/Building Society
Address	
	Postcode

Name(s) of account holder(s)

Branch sort code	Bank/Building Society account number

Reference

Instruction to your Bank/Building Society

Please pay The Bible Reading Fellowship Direct Debits from the account detailed in this instruction, subject to the safeguards assured by the Direct Debit Guarantee.
I understand that this instruction may remain with The Bible Reading Fellowship and, if so, details will be passed electronically to my bank/building society.

Signature(s)
Date

Banks and Building Societies may not accept Direct Debit instructions for some types of account.

This page is intentionally left blank.